Melbourne Bound

First published in 2016 by Barbara Greenwood
ISBN 978-1-5272-0021-0
Typesetting and layout by Carnegie Book Production, Lancaster
Typeset in 10.5pt on 14pt Chaparral Pro.
Printed in the UK by Cambrian Printers

Melbourne Bound

From the Neb to the Yarra

Barbara Greenwood

To Collette
best wishes from
Barbara

Dedication

Lt. Col. Brian Mylchreest
L.V.O., O.B.E., T.D., J.P.
1916–2014

I dedicate this book to my Uncle, Brian Mylchreest, a proud Manxman whose research into Peel sailing boats (*Peveril* in particular) stimulated me to embark on this project.

Barbara Greenwood, 2016

Foreword

I WAS HONOURED TO be asked to write this foreword as over the years I have developed a friendship with three generations of the Mylchreest family and the late Colonel Brian Mylchreest furnished me with the information upon which I based the book *Peel – a Slice of Time*, the first book produced under the auspices of Peel Heritage Trust's publishing arm *Peel City Guardian*, this book being another P.H.T. publishing venture.

They say that 'big oaks from small acorns grow' and I feel correct in saying that like an acorn the stories of *Vixen* and *Peveril* have grown since Barbara first embarked upon this project, her diligent research knowing no bounds; although this is the third book involving the Mylchreests – the first being Brian's *The Diamond King* published in 1993 – this is, in fact, a prequel!

Manxmen have always been wont to travel; perhaps like sheepdogs hardwired for their task, it has come down through our genes – part of our Viking heritage – who knows? It is amazing how many countries in the world you may visit and find traces of our forebears.

To the outside world it may seem remarkable that a small group of Manxmen should embark upon a journey south from their home town of Peel to the other side of the world in a boat they constructed in a local shipyard; but to them it was just another voyage and, after all, they were confident in their abilities as both sailors and navigators. So confident were they in their vessels that they embarked upon, and completed, this antipodean adventure not once but twice!

This description of both expeditions furnishes us with the information as to how these travels were undertaken, the men involved, and the goods they carried with them, how they fared in the Southern Hemisphere, and their Manx descendants living there today.

As you delve into this book you will come to appreciate their determination to succeed in everything they undertook; hardly surprising then that one of the Mylchreest family roamed the world to become the owner of his own diamond mines in South Africa and one of the Island's richest men – Joe Mylchreest 'The Diamond King' – just one more apprentice boat builder from Peel.

I'm sure that as you read this account (be you from the Northern or Southern Hemisphere) you will come to admire the wanderings of these modest Manxmen.

If you are connected to any of them you can rejoice in your genealogy; who knows, perhaps you too will feel the need to roam.

Enjoy.

Bill Quine, Peel Heritage Trust, 2016

Contents

List of Illustrations

Introduction

BY THEIR VERY nature islands have always bred seafarers. The Isle of Man situated in the middle of the Irish Sea is no exception and the lure of the sea is no doubt in the Viking blood of many Manxmen. During the nineteenth century the need to support an increasing population sent many Manx adventurers overseas, fuelled by stories of gold and untold riches in Australia and elsewhere.

Peel was the main ship building town on the west coast of the Isle of Man. This is the story of two Peel-built boats that made the journey to Australia: *Vixen* (1851–64), which sailed to Australia in 1853, was a 93 ton schooner and *Peveril* (1848–85) a 59 ton cutter and which sailed to Australia in 1854. The partial history of both boats has been written over the years and the memories of the *Vixen* men lived well on into the twentieth century. *Peveril* is less well remembered in the Isle of Man, possibly because she had a smaller crew and never returned to her native shores. She nevertheless had an eventful history in Australian waters.

My interest in *Peveril* is that her first Master was John Mylchreest (1805–49), my two times great grandfather. Two of his sons, Thomas (1830–92) and John (1832–88) were on the epic Australian voyage in 1854. A younger son Joseph (1839–96) was only 15 when *Peveril* left Peel or else surely he would have gone too. Instead he didn't start his travels until 1858 when he initially joined his brothers in Australia before travelling to New Zealand, North America and South America seeking his fortune. He finally ended up in Kimberley, South Africa in a more or less penniless state in 1876. Within 12 short years his luck changed dramatically and he returned to Peel a wealthy man universally known as 'The Diamond King'.

My Uncle, Brian Mylchreest, researched his grandfather, the Diamond King, extensively (Mylchreest, 1993). He had also been trying to find the story behind *Peveril* since the 1950s. He included much of this in a privately circulated work (Mylchreest, 1989). However it has been only recently that on-line resources, particularly newspapers, have become available and which make researching nineteenth-century history easier (see sources). Consequently this work started out as an update of Brian's work based on recent findings. It soon became clear (prompted by Bill Quine and Vic Bates of the Peel Heritage Trust) that although the *Vixen* story is not directly linked to that of *Peveril*, the overlap is substantial.

So these two small boats, built on the River Neb in Peel, Isle of Man both made the hazardous journey to the River Yarra in Melbourne, Australia. This is their story.

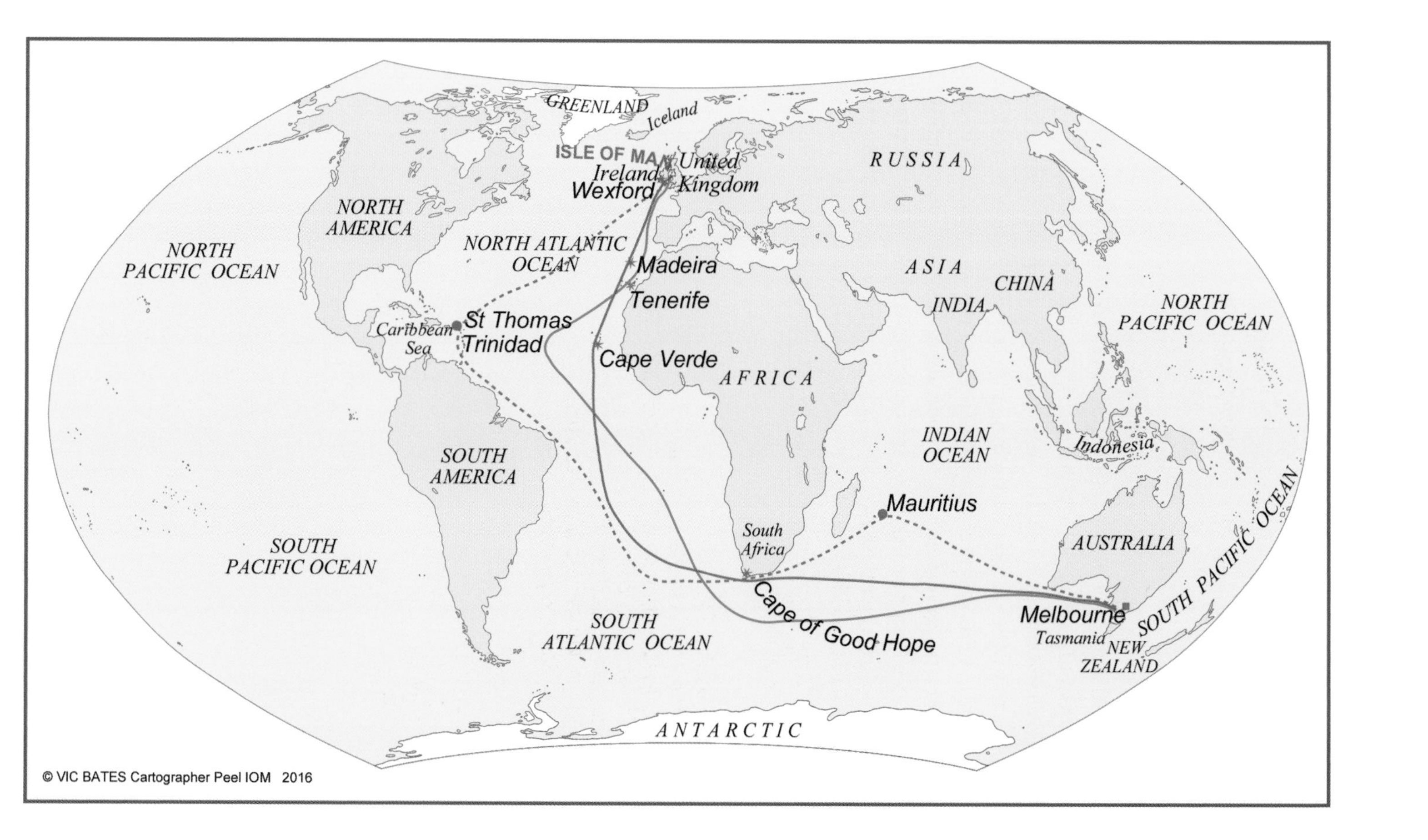
GREENLAND
Iceland
ISLE OF MAN
Ireland
Wexford
United Kingdom
RUSSIA
NORTH AMERICA
NORTH PACIFIC OCEAN
NORTH ATLANTIC OCEAN
Madeira
Tenerife
St Thomas
Trinidad
Caribbean Sea
Cape Verde
AFRICA
ASIA
CHINA
INDIA
NORTH PACIFIC OCEAN
INDIAN OCEAN
Indonesia
SOUTH AMERICA
Mauritius
South Africa
AUSTRALIA
SOUTH PACIFIC OCEAN
SOUTH PACIFIC OCEAN
SOUTH ATLANTIC OCEAN
Cape of Good Hope
Melbourne
Tasmania
NEW ZEALAND
ANTARCTIC
© VIC BATES Cartographer Peel IOM 2016

THE PEVERIL
Departed Peel 24th March 1854
Arrived Melbourne 5th August 1854 (4 months and 12 days)
No land sighted between Tenerife and Australia
Never returned to Peel
——— *Outward journey to Australia*

THE VIXEN
Departed Peel on 26th January 1853
Arrived Melbourne 3rd May 1853 (92 days)
✳ *Places visited on outward journey*
● *Places visited on return journey*
——— *Outward journey to Australia*
- - - - - *Return journey to Peel*

Fig 1 Map of the Voyages of *Vixen* and *Peveril*, with legend

Pre-1850 Peel

PEEL CASTLE ON St Patrick's Isle and Peel Town or Purt ny h-Inshey (Harbour of the Island) have led parallel but distinct identities throughout historic times. Whilst the castle had its military and ecclesiastical priorities, the town always turned to the sea for its livelihood. This existed until the twentieth century. Mid-nineteenth-century Peel was a bustling place of over 3000 people mostly employed in fishing, trading, shipbuilding and ancillary industries (fish curing, rope making etc.). The town plan was rather haphazard with roads converging on Market Place but with houses mixed with smithies, stables, bakeries and other premises (Fig 2). Shipbuilding developed along the River Neb and Peel-built schooners were trading throughout Europe and the Mediterranean whilst Peel fishing boats sought mackerel off Kinsale in Ireland or followed the herring as far away as Shetland.

Slater's Directory (1857) states that 'The Port has the convenience of a good quay, erected in 1810 with a light-house at its extremity, and a jetty of substantial masonry was constructed in 1830. The herring fishery may be considered the staple of Peel; there are however, several other branches of some consequences, as ship and boat-building, brewing, tanning, sail-making etc.'

As well as being good fishermen, Peel men were skilled navigators as many of the ships' Masters had trained at Gawne's School of Navigation in the town (Fig 3 and number 17, Fig 2). This operated from the 1820s to the 1850s by John Gawne who taught navigation to young men who

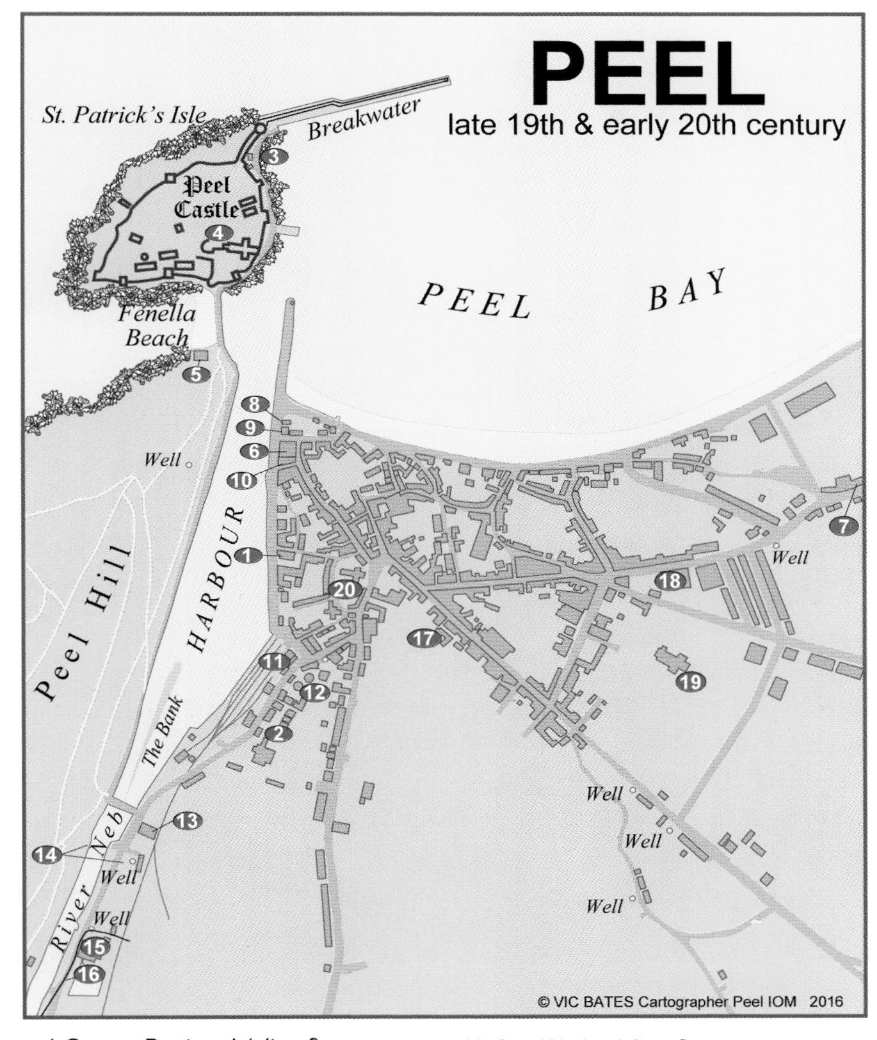

1 Graves Boatyard *(site of)*
2 Graves Saw Mill *(site of)*
3 Lifeboat House
4 St German's Cathedral *(ruin)*
5 Fenella Hotel *(site of)*
6 Peveril Public House
7 Ballarat Terrace
8 Sailors' Shelter
9 Harbourmaster's Office
10 Courthouse *(now Leece Museum)*
11 Railway Station *(now House of Mannanan)*
12 Gas Works *(site of)*
13 Moore's Kipper House
14 Thomas Watson's Boatyard *(site of)*
15 Thomas Watson's Saw Mill *(site of)*
16 Brickworks Plateway *(site of)*
17 Gawne's School of Navigation *(now private house)*
18 Peel Clothworkers' School *(now community hall)*
19 Church of St German *(now Cathedral)*
20 St Peters Church *(ruin)*

Fig 2 Map of Peel in the late nineteenth and early twentieth century

Fig 3 Gawne's School of Navigation. © Vic Bates

attended evening classes to be coached for their Master's tickets. Gawne's school had its origins in Moore's Mathematical School which was founded in 1763 and was for many years the centre of learning on the Island.

The Mylchreest family can trace its origin in Peel through many generations. John Mylchreest (1805–49) was born in Peel in 1805 and married Christian Moore in 1825. Although no doubt with historic relations he is not thought to be directly connected to the earliest burial in the churchyard of St Peter in Market Place (number 20, Fig 2). This was one Wm Mylkreest who died on 16 August 1698. John and Christian set

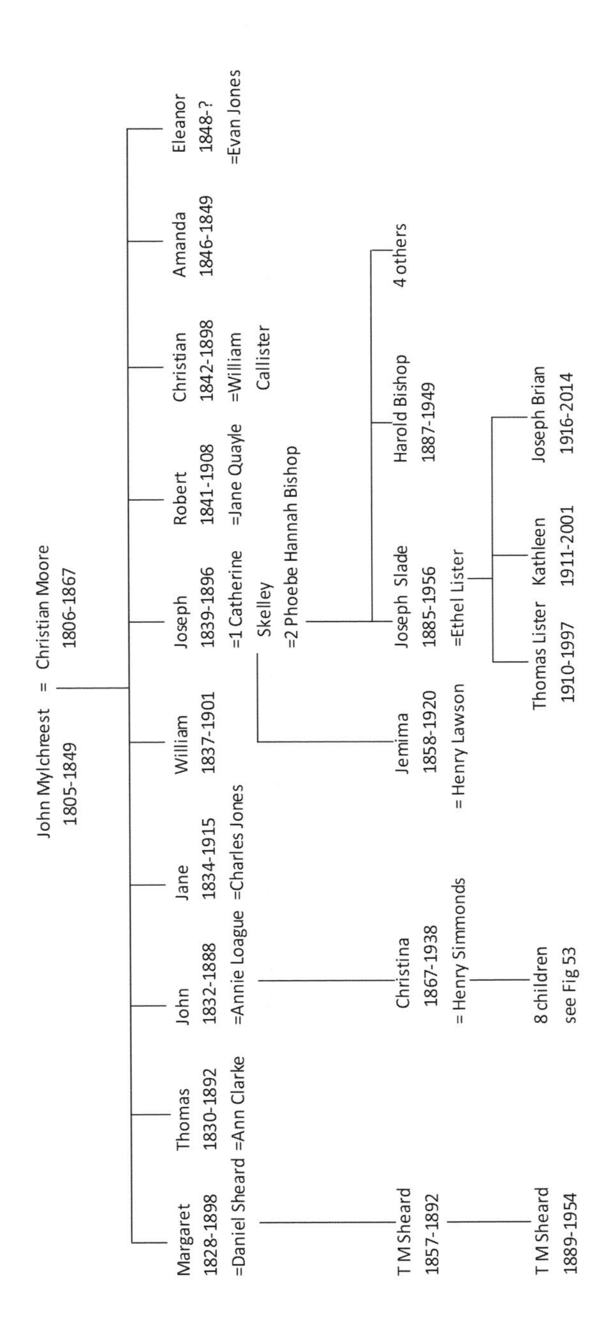

Fig 4 Simplified tree showing the descendants of John Mylchreest (1805–49)

up home on Strand Street and were living there at the time of the 1841 census with their children Margaret (born 1828), Thomas (born 1830), John (born 1832), Jane (born 1834), William (born 1837) and Joseph (born 1839). They were later joined by Robert (born 1841), Christian (born 1842), Amanda (born 1846) and Eleanor (born 1848).

John Mylchreest was a skilled mariner and had his first command at the age of 21 on the *Lively*, a 23 ton fishing smack built in Douglas in 1804. Transferred to the Peel registry in 1825, *Lively* was owned by Thomas Kaighen, John Kaighen, William Quilliam (all Peel fishermen), John Cowley (Peel shoemaker) and Thomas Shimmin (Manchester labourer). He followed this with commands of the *Brazils* (1833), and the *Etty and Peggy* (1838) before becoming Master of *Peveril 1* in 1840. *Peveril 1* was a newly built 35 ton fishing smack of which John was a part owner along with William Kinley, Robert Moore (both Peel advocates), Henry and Thomas Graves (sailmaker), William Cain and Richard Cowley (Peel farmers). She was sold and transferred to the Douglas registry in 1848 when *Peveril 2* was built in Peel. After *Peveril 2* went to Australia, a third *Peveril* was built in Peel in 1869 and was a 66 ton 2-masted schooner built and owned by Daniel Sheard and H. T. Graves. She was stranded at Laxey and broken up in 1891. Thus the name *Peveril* overlapped with the Isle of Man Steam Packet Company's *Peveril*, a screw steamer built in Barrow-in -Furness in 1884. Her 15 year career with the IOMSPCo ended in 1899 when she sank off Douglas Head after a collision with the steam ship *Monarch*. There was no loss of life but all cargo was lost including a number of pictures by Archibald Knox.

Fig 5 Peel in *c.* 1890. Courtesy of Peel Heritage Trust

Peveril 2 (hereafter just called *Peveril*) was a 59 ton fishing smack built of oak and fir (probably a species of pine) in Henry Graves' Peel yard in 1848 (number 1, Fig 2). She was registered (number 31635) on 2 May 1848, single masted and cutter rigged, measuring 56ft long and 19ft beam. The owners listed her in Lloyds Register of British and Foreign Shipping from 1849 to 1856. The 64 shares were equally divided between the eight owners viz:

Henry Graves	Peel	Sailmaker
Thomas Joshua Graves	Peel	Sailmaker
Robert John Moore	Peel	Advocate
Henry Maddrell Graves	Peel	Carpenter
John Mylchreest	Peel	Master Mariner
William Cain	Peel	Farmer
Henry Gill	Douglas	Master Mariner
Robert Watson	Manchester	Fishmonger

Fig 5A Modern Peel harbour © Barbara Greenwood
Graves' Yard (now the Boatyard restaurant) is indicated by arrows in this picture and in Figure 5. The courthouse (now the Leece Museum) is clearly seen on the left of both pictures (number 10, Fig 2), as is the tower of St Peter's Church (number 20, Fig 2)

Fig 6 *Peveril* leaving Peel in 1854. From a watercolour by Peter Hearsey. Courtesy of the Mylchreest family

Although the Graves family originally came from Yorkshire, their presence in Peel had a considerable effect on the economy and social history of the town. It was a large family, many of whom have bearing on the *Vixen* and *Peveril* stories, so it is worth summarising the links. Henry Graves (*c.* 1744 – 1797) had two sons John Thomas (1781–1833) and Thomas Joshua (1786–1846). Two of John Thomas' and three of Thomas Joshua's sons are of interest here. Henry Maddrell (1820–92) and Robert (1825–91) were the sons of John Thomas. Henry Maddrell Graves was a carpenter who sailed on *Vixen* and owned 8 shares in *Peveril*. After six years in Australia he returned to Peel. Of great significance is a type-written document describing the building, fitting out and provisioning of *Vixen*, together with extracts from Henry's diary of the first part of the voyage to Melbourne. A copy is in the possession of Bill Quine who acquired it from Ean Wood shortly before his death in 2010. It is believed to have belonged to Ean's grandparents Joseph and Marion Wood of Tynwald Street, Peel. It is unsigned and undated but refers to Neakle and Watterson's yard still operating so must pre-date 1939 when the yard closed. It forms part of a longer article in the Isle of Man Natural History and Antiquarian Society Journal (Graves, 1968) which gives a fascinating insight into nineteenth-century Peel as well as the *Vixen* story.

Henry Maddrell's brother was Robert who also sailed on *Vixen*. Seemingly he had married Elizabeth Kelly in 1850 but doesn't appear to have returned from Australia to his wife and two young children.

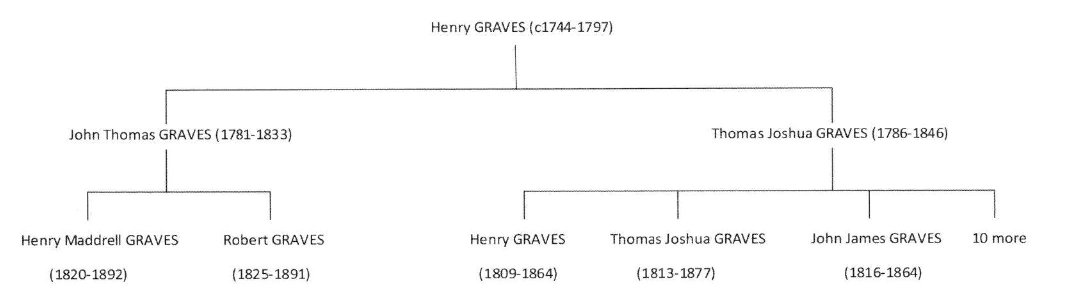

Fig 7 Simplified tree showing the Graves family of Peel

Three sons of Thomas Joshua are noteworthy: Henry (1809–64), Thomas Joshua (1813–77) and John James (1816–64). Thomas Joshua owned 8 shares in both *Vixen* and *Peveril*. He sailed on *Vixen* and returned to a successful career as sailmaker and ship owner in Peel. His grave in Peel new cemetery depicts *Vixen* leaving Peel in 1853. His brother John James also sailed on *Vixen* and returned about 1860 to work in the family shipyard. This leaves Henry who never left Peel but whose ship building business was by far the largest there. At one time he had three yards in Peel and owned 16 shares in *Vixen* and 8 in *Peveril*, both of which had been built in his yards. Most likely this was the harbour-side one, now the site of the Boatyard restaurant (Figs 5 and 5A; number 1, Fig 2).

Another family with strong links to the story are the Watsons. Thomas Watson's yard (number 14, Fig 2) built many interesting Peel boats in the 1890s such as *Phoebe* (Quine & Bates, 2011). Thomas was the son of Samuel Watson, a Peel mariner born in Ireland in *c.* 1801. It is suggested that Samuel had two brothers, William (born Ireland *c.* 1806) who farmed Ballaspet in Patrick and Robert (born Ireland *c.* 1804) who was a Manchester fishmonger. Robert owned 16 shares in *Vixen* and 8 in *Peveril*

Fig 8 Tom Sheard (right) and his cousin Harold Mylchreest © R. A.Sheard

whilst Samuel and William had 8 shares each in the two-masted smack *Bloomer* (of which Samuel was also Master). At 23 tons, *Bloomer* was only small but she adds an interesting piece to the jigsaw. The registry says she was built in Peel by Daniel Sheard in 1852. Daniel, a ships' carpenter, didn't have a yard of his own at that time so must have constructed *Bloomer* on spare ground or at his lodgings which just happened to be with the Mylchreest family. Christian, by then a widow, bought 8 shares in *Bloomer*, and her eldest daughter Margaret went on to marry Daniel. Their grandson was Thomas Mylchreest Sheard who in 1922 was the first Manxman to win a TT race (Fig 8).

Bloomer herself traded and fished the Irish Sea for many years before being stranded on Stranraer beach and broken up in 1881. There is another William Watson born in Patrick in 1829, a mariner and Master of another Peel built schooner, the *Ark*. He may have been a relation.

Returning to *Peveril*, regrettably her log has been lost, but it is possible to track many of her pre-1854 voyages through local newspapers and shipping intelligence. It seems she was first employed in the Mediterranean fruit trade with the *Manx Sun* reporting on 8 November 1848:

> *The* Peveril, *John Mylchreest master, belonging to Peel has made a splendid trip from Malaga to Dublin, being the second vessel that has arrived there out of above twenty that sailed at the same time. So much for Peel smacks!*

A local news report in the *Manx Sun* two years later (14 December 1850) also reported the success of Peel smacks in the fruit trade:

> *The* Union, *H. Gell from Seville, has arrived at Leith; the* Eclipse, *J. Gell from Seville, at Hull, the* Comet, *T. Gell from Seville at Liverpool, ran from Cape St Vincent to Liverpool in five days, all fruit laden; the* Peveril, *T. Mylchreest, from Peel to Bayonne.*

Presumably the voyage from Seville was down the Guadalquivir River.

Peveril's Bayonne voyage was with a cargo of flour, having earlier arrived in Liverpool with fruit from Malaga, as reported in the *Mona's Herald* for 13 November 1850:

> *There are at present eight vessels belonging to Peel at foreign ports principally employed in the fruit trade. Such a circumstance is without parallel in the history of insular shipping, and reflects great credit on the little town of Peel.*

There was a market for fresh fruit throughout the year, especially in the more affluent parts of industrial Britain. Home production in the summer months was usually sufficient but in the winter months supplies had to be brought in from elsewhere. The Mediterranean fruit trade proved most profitable and many Manx boats joined this fleet. It was timed especially to provide fresh fruit for the Christmas market. Oranges, lemons, pineapples, dates etc. were regularly brought to Britain from the Mediterranean and the Azores. The trade was further helped by the repeal of the Corn Laws in 1846 which removed duty on fruit from these areas.

Whilst the fruit trade was primarily a winter activity, fishing occupied the summer months. It was in the summer of 1849 that tragedy struck the *Peveril*. Captain John Mylchreest and his crew (including his 19 year old son Thomas) left Peel for the fishing grounds off Kinsale, south of Cork, but John died on the passage. It has not been possible to determine

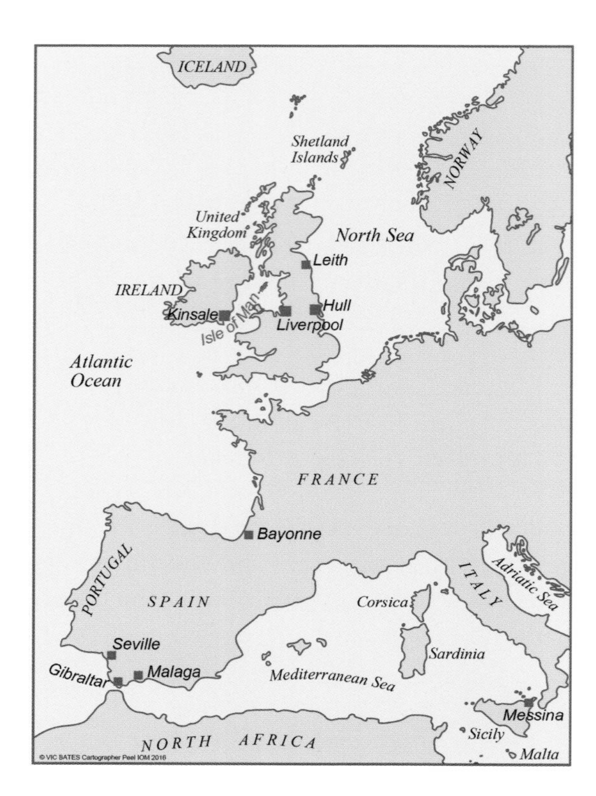

Fig 9 Map of Europe showing the position of the Isle of Man with British and European ports

the circumstances of his death. Did he drown or did he die of injury or natural causes? Searches of the Irish records, newspapers and burials have all proved negative and surprisingly the Manx newspapers make no mention of it on *Peveril*'s return to Peel on 13 August 1849. He is not buried in the Peel grave with his wife Christian, son Thomas and his wife Ann (although there is space left for an inscription on the headstone, Figs 54 and 55).

Thomas was confirmed as the new Master on 1 September 1849 and he re-commenced trading with a voyage to Glasgow on 5 September. John didn't leave a will, but had some property, including the part share of *Peveril*, so Letters of Administration were taken out and the entry in the Ecclesiastical Court Book reads:

> *John Mylchreest departed this life sometime on or about the month of August 1849 at Cork. Administration granted to Christian (widow) and*

Daniel Sheard (son in law). William Garrett, advocate, at an Ecclesiastical Court at Kirk Michael 15th December 1853.

John's share in *Peveril* was accordingly transferred to Christian on 31 March 1854, and Thomas continued as Master, joined in the crew by his younger brother John. Thomas, although young, was as skilled a mariner as his father and *Peveril* continued fishing and trading up to the time she left for Australia as this entry in the *Manx Sun* for 27 August 1853 testifies:

The spirited Peel ship-owners continue to engage in new descriptions of trades with their smacks of repute. The Peveril, *Mylchreest master, left for Iceland on the 10th May and returned on the 21st of this month with a choice cargo of codfish etc, of about 40 tons.*

The Rush for Gold

NO DOUBT SOME Peel men were lured to California in the 1849 goldrush, but it is events in Australia that are of particular interest here. Until 1849 Port Phillip District was part of New South Wales and when Victoria became an independent colony there was fierce rivalry between the two. So when gold was discovered in New South Wales in February 1851, Victoria didn't want to be left behind, especially as men were leaving Victoria to go to the New South Wales diggings. Governor La Trobe offered a 200 guinea reward for anyone finding gold within 200 miles (322 km) of Melbourne.

Rumours of gold findings in the Ballarat area had been circulating for a while but the first registered gold discovery was made at Clunes some 21 miles (35 km) north of Ballarat. James William Esmond claimed the reward after discovering the first marketable gold on Donald Cameron's station on 1 July 1851. This find which was heralded in the *Geelong Advertiser* of 25 July 1851 (see Appendix 1), along with those at Anderson's Creek, Warrandyte and Bununyong, triggered the Great Victorian Goldrush. The population of Victoria trebled from 77,000 in 1851 to 237,000 in 1854 and peaked at 411,000. Whilst many migrants came from elsewhere in Australia, the vast majority came from overseas, primarily Britain. Chinese gold seekers, mostly from southern China, were also significant participants in the goldrush. At one stage in the late 1850s they accounted for one in ten of the Victorian population. For further information about the Victorian goldrush see Flett (1970) and Serle (1963).

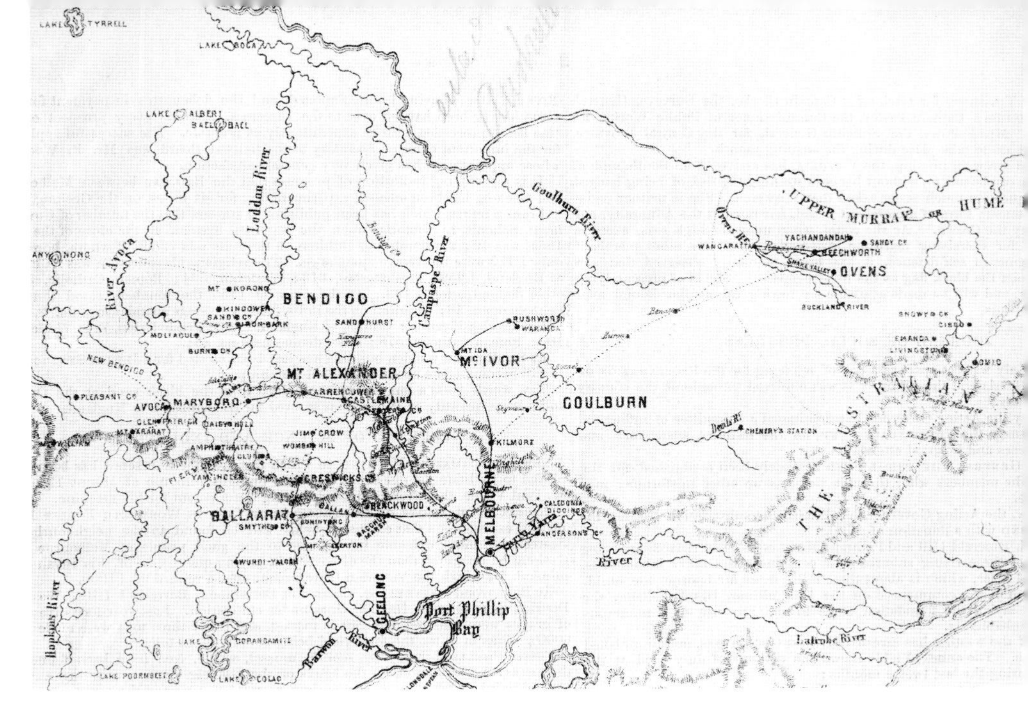

Fig 10 Map of the goldfields of Victoria. Wood engraving by George Slater, *The Newsletter of Australasia*, August 1856. Courtesy of the State Library of Victoria

Melbourne had only been settled by Europeans less than ten years before gold was found. Explorers from Tasmania went up the Yarra River and founded the town, then known as Port Philip. At the time the goldrush started, there was very little infrastructure and the town consisted of a collection of huts and tents, woefully inadequate for the number of migrants arriving (Fig 11). The new migrants would have

Fig 11 Canvas Town outside Melbourne, on the shores of Hobson's Bay, 1853. Wood engraving from a sketch by S. T. Gill. Published in *Illustrated Australian News* 25 June 1887. Courtesy of the State Library of Victoria

Fig 12 Diggers on road to Bendigo, about 1853. Watercolour by S. T. Gill. Courtesy of the State Library of Victoria

arrived in Melbourne full of expectation then had to make their way to the goldfields, often totally ignorant of what lay ahead of them.

The more affluent would have travelled by coach or bullock wagon but the vast majority would have walked pushing their possessions in a cart or carrying them on their backs (Fig 12). The roads were not made up so travel was exceedingly difficult – hot, dry and dusty in summer; wet and muddy in winter. On arrival at the goldfields the early gold seekers would have used cradles and pans to separate alluvial gold from the mixture of gravel and water. Only later as the alluvial gold was exhausted would

Fig 13 Zealous gold diggers, Castlemaine 1852. Watercolour by S. T. Gill. Courtesy of the State Library of Victoria

Fig 14 Ballarat Flat from the Black Hill. Steel engraving by J. Tingle. *Published in Victoria Illustrated* (1857). Courtesy of the State Library of Victoria

mining begin which required several diggers to work together in co-operation. Often gold digging involved the whole family (Fig 13).

Life in the tented cities on the goldfields was harsh in the beginning and there are many first-hand accounts of the trials and tribulations of the miners, as well as the potential lucrative rewards. Such an example is the letter received by Mr R. Crossley of South Castle Street, Liverpool from his brother Mr E. W. Crossley dated Christmas Day 1851 from Geelong. It was published in the *Mona's Herald* of 5 May 1852. The full article is given in Appendix 2.

> *As I have now returned from my second excursion at gold digging, I shall give you just some little idea of the success of myself and the generality of the diggers in this auriferous region. Set to work [in the Mount Alexander field], rigged the cradle; got two ounces out of the first cartload; washed about four loads on the Tuesday, which weighed with the proceeds of Wednesday, gave us for the day and a half 72*

ounces, including a splendid nugget of 40 ounces, about as large as a man's hand stretched out, and something in the same shape, varying in thickness from a half to a quarter of an inch; also a fine specimen in orange-coloured quartz, of the value of about 30s in gold. This looked like a good yield, which continued for ten days; and at the expiration of about five weeks from starting we again returned to town to spend the Christmas, with gold to the value of £150 each. In about ten days' time we start again, and I have no doubt of our success being as good or better than previous. I have a thousand pounds in my pocket, and I have never yet regretted the day that I left England. Last week over a ton of gold came down from Mount Alexander, under escort, independent of what came down by private parties, which might be estimated at half a ton, by parties coming down to spend Christmas.

Fig 15 Gold License [sic] no. 206. Issued to Peter Lalor, October 1853 and valid for the month of November. Issued by Commissioner J. K. Hood. This is a mock up produced by the Ballarat Historical Society, it appears to have been copied from the Gold License [sic] of George Hogarth in W. B. Withers' book *History of Ballarat*, 1887. Courtesy of the State Library of Victoria

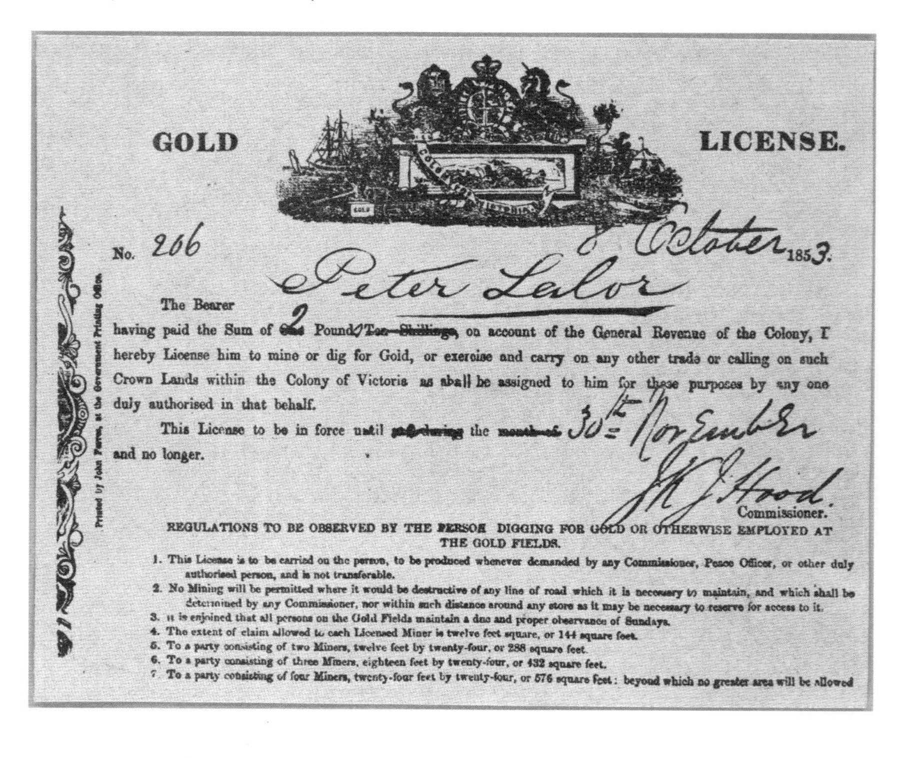

GOLD LICENSE.

No. 206 8 October 1853.

The Bearer Peter Lalor

having paid the Sum of ~~One~~ 2 Pound ~~Ten Shillings~~, on account of the General Revenue of the Colony, I hereby License him to mine or dig for Gold, or exercise and carry on any other trade or calling on such Crown Lands within the Colony of Victoria as shall be assigned to him for these purposes by any one duly authorised in that behalf.

This License to be in force until ~~for during~~ the ~~month of~~ 30th November and no longer.

J K J Hood.
Commissioner.

Printed by John Ferres, at the Government Printing Office.

REGULATIONS TO BE OBSERVED BY THE PERSON DIGGING FOR GOLD OR OTHERWISE EMPLOYED AT THE GOLD FIELDS.

1. This License is to be carried on the person, to be produced whenever demanded by any Commissioner, Peace Officer, or other duly authorised person, and is not transferable.
2. No Mining will be permitted where it would be destructive of any line of road which it is necessary to maintain, and which shall be determined by any Commissioner, nor within such distance around any store as it may be necessary to reserve for access to it.
3. It is enjoined that all persons on the Gold Fields maintain a due and proper observance of Sundays.
4. The extent of claim allowed to each Licensed Miner is twelve feet square, or 144 square feet.
5. To a party consisting of two Miners, twelve feet by twenty-four, or 288 square feet.
6. To a party consisting of three Miners, eighteen feet by twenty-four, or 432 square feet.
7. To a party consisting of four Miners, twenty-four feet by twenty-four, or 576 square feet: beyond which no greater area will be allowed

Fig 16 The License [sic] Inspected. Watercolour by S. T. Gill (1818–80). Courtesy of the State Library of Victoria

Mr Crossley states that 'at the present no lynch law is in vogue' but predicts this will change when 'the tide of emigration sets in'. This was indeed the case and the diggings were pretty lawless places. The so-called 'police' enforced ruthless checks on mining licences whilst lining their own pockets at the same time (Figs 15 and 16).

The miners took matters into their own hands in November 1854 and barricaded themselves into a stockade at the Eureka Mine. This was over-run by Government troops and more than 30 miners lost their lives. The Eureka rebellion however did have its effect and a fairer system of licensing ensued.

The *Peel City Guardian* of 3 February 1912 states that:

> *Those gold fever days of the eighteen fifties were wild and adventurous. Men carried their lives in their hands. The late Mr John Cain of Ballaquane often used to supply vivid word pictures of the scenes at the diggings. He was at Ballarat when the rebellion occurred. Many of the* Vixen's *crew were at the diggings in 1856, the* annus mirabilis *of the gold workings. In that year sheep were left unshorn, corn unreaped, and ships without sailors.*

Fig 17 The City Hall and Craig's Hotel, Ballarat, *c*. 1890. Photograph by Charles Rudd. Courtesy of the State Library of Victoria

However, by the end of the decade Ballarat had grown into a prominent town with magnificent Victorian buildings lining wide tree-lined avenues.

The itinerant nature of the miners' lives meant it was difficult to assess the number of them there at any one time, but upwards of 160,000 were thought to have been there at the peak (1856). This was also the time when some 70,000 ounces of gold per week were being deposited in the Melbourne Treasury (Fig 18). By 1896 it is estimated that over 61 million ounces of gold had been found in Victoria.

Today, Sovereign Hill open air museum in Ballarat gives a wonderful idea of what life must have been like in the first ten years of the goldrush (Fig 19).

By the beginning of 1852 word of the discoveries was reaching Britain, and the Manx papers were reporting the events, such as the *Mona's Herald*, 25 February 1852:

> *Important News from the Gold Diggings of Australia*

and the *Manx Sun*, 27 March 1852:

> *The Gold Mines of Australia: Extraordinary Success*

Fig 18 The Treasury, Melbourne, 1854. Coloured lithograph by S. T. Gill (1818–80). Courtesy of the State Library of Victoria

Fig 19 Sovereign Hill open air museum in Ballarat recreates goldfield life of the 1850s. © Barbara Greenwood

A letter from Thomas Gawne dated 12 November 1851 was published in the *Mona's Herald* of 12 May 1852 (the full letter is given in Appendix 3). In it he speaks of the great opportunities for Manxmen in Victoria and says:

> *All seasons of the year answer to come here. Cashen says even a fishing luggar might make the passage. My advice is to one intending coming here, to look for a good captain and officers, which is of the greatest moment: they will take care to have a good ship. A Farmer may find employment here in all the branches, excepting manuring and limeing, which will pay very well those that will attend to it. As to produce, we can scarcely grow enough. A labouring man that is sober and active, will get from £25 to £30 a year. The gold is 60 miles from Geelong, and all sorts of people are gone there: they get from 1 to 12 oz. per week, and some lbs. weight. There is a government escort with mounted police comes down twice a week. What would answer the best purpose would be a number of Manx to come all together and form a colony: it would make people always at home.*

Shortly afterwards advertisements for sailings to Melbourne and the gold diggings started appearing in the press. For example the *City of Lincoln* (1200 tons) would carry steerage passengers from Liverpool to Melbourne for £15 and £45 for First Class.

At this point it might be useful to compare the relative value of wages in 1851 although this is very imprecise and only an average. For example many agricultural labourers in Britain may only have been employed seasonally or else their regular wages might be supplemented at harvest time etc.

Agricultural Labourer	£30
Skilled worker in shipbuilding	£64
Skilled worker in the building trade	£66
Clergyman	£267
Engineer	£479
Solicitor	£1837

Fig 20 Average wages in 1850 (after Williamson, 1982)

Thus the steerage passage to Melbourne would cost approximately half what an agricultural labourer might expect to earn in a year whilst the £150 Mr Crossley and his colleagues each earned in five weeks of digging would seem like untold riches (see Appendix 2).

Just one week after the Clunes gold find was reported, the schooner *Vixen* was launched from Henry Graves' yard in Peel. At 93 tons registered and capable of carrying 'about 150 tons', she was the largest vessel built in Peel up to that date.

> *This vessel, which is coppered, and built of the best description of materials, reflects great credit on Mr Graves, and is intended for the Mediterranean fruit trade.*
> *Manx Sun 2 August 1851*

She was owned jointly by:

Henry Graves	Peel	Shipbuilder	16 shares
Thomas Cubbon	Patrick	Mariner (Master)	4 shares
Daniel McIntosh	Campbeltown, Argyll	Fisherman	8 shares
Thomas Joshua Graves	Peel	Sailmaker	8 shares
Henry Watterson	Peel	Mariner	4 shares
Robert Watson	Manchester	Fishmonger	16 shares
William Mackenzie	Campbeltown, Argyll	Fisherman	8 shares

The two Campbeltown fishermen had links with Peel and Daniel was married to a Manx girl. One of their sons was named John Graves McIntosh. Both men sold their shares in *Vixen* immediately prior to her sailing to Australia in January 1853.

One of *Vixen's* first voyages was from Peel to Cardiff where upon arrival Captain Cubbon wrote to the owners who published the letter in *Mona's Herald* of 3 September 1851:

> *We left the Calf of Man at 10 o'clock on Wednesday evening and got to Swansea at 6 o'clock on Thursday evening. We were in company with several schooners and brigs, which we passed as if lying to. There were two Holyhead clippers with us, and we left them out of sight. The pilots here would not believe that the like could be built in the Island.*

She took a cargo of iron from Cardiff to Messina, Italy, returning to Liverpool with fruit. Thereafter several journeys between the Mediterranean and Irish Sea ports, and finally back to Peel on 13 October 1852.

With all the gold reports coming to the Island from Australia, it is small wonder that the men of Peel wanted to be part of the action. Consequently 37 of them planned a co-operative venture to charter *Vixen* and sail to Melbourne. Once there, they would work together in the diggings, share their fortune and return home wealthy men. This was a fairly radical plan; it is well documented and it appears there may have been some formal arrangement as reported in the *Manx Sun* of 16 October 1852:

> *It is currently rumoured and on enquiry we find the report to have some foundation that a party of Peel [20 to 30] adventurers intend [chartering] a smart vessel and proceeding direct to Australia.... The parties to bind themselves by indenture, to certain articles, for two years.... To have one common fund, share and share alike.*

Then in the *Manx Sun* of 25 December 1852:

> *The schooner* Vixen *of Peel, which has for some weeks past been undergoing alterations for increased accommodation, is expected to be ready to sail the first week in January from that port direct for Australia, with thirty five adventurers who intend trying their fortune at the gold diggings.*

The 35 adventurers would have excluded the Master, Captain Thomas Cubbon and navigator, Thomas Corlett of Dalby. Others of the 35 would have been sailors but perhaps they were also part of the co-operative.

An interesting account of the venture is given in the *Manx Sun* of 5 September 1903 which prints an extensive obituary of Evan Gell, one of the original adventurers. The full obituary is given in Appendix 4, and a summary states:

> *Mr Gell told of the experiment at Socialism many times. Before the emigrants of the* Vixen *left Peel they arranged that for twelve months in the new country they would put all wages in one purse, and divide equally after all expenses had been paid. Another part*

of the socialistic scheme was that the 37 cargoed the Vixen *with wheelbarrows, picks, shovels, iron bars (for horse shoes etc), and last but not least, red Manx salt herrings, of which they had not a few barrels. All the above were sold at auction on arrival and realised such fancy prices that the voyage only cost them £2 each.*

Graves (1968) has details of the cash paid on account for the fitting out of *Vixen*. This includes provisions for the voyage, items to set up the adventurers at the diggings and freight that they planned to sell on arrival. However it is very difficult to distinguish between the categories. For example £16 12*s*. 6*d*. was paid to E. Edwards for picks but does not give any quantity. Were these freight or bought on behalf of the co-operative? How many horseshoes could have been bought from Richard Shimmin for £7 7*s*.? Presumably Richard is the blacksmith living in Douglas Street, Peel who also supplied a cart for £1 10*s*. His next door neighbour was John Garrett, saddler, who supplied harness to the value of £7 10*s*.

Eight of the adventurers were paid for 'work' prior to leaving Peel. Was this to do with fitting out prior to the voyage or payment in advance for sailing the vessel to Australia?

Unfortunately there is no income account, so there is no way of knowing who financed the purchases. Did the adventurers pay for their provisions and freight or did the owners underwrite it? How much did the adventurers pay for the charter? All we know is that a total of £1,018 12*s*. 7½ *d*. was paid out before *Vixen* left Peel on 26 January 1853.

The Journey Out

WHEN *VIXEN* SAILED on 26 January 1853, it was probably the most memorable day in the history of Peel to that date (Fig 21). The build-up had been considerable and even a day's delay due to bad tides did not diminish the enthusiasm. People came from all over the Island, schools were closed and guns primed to signal her departure. *Vixen's* departure is noted in the Shipping Intelligence of the *Manx Sun* of 29 January. There is a further account in the *Manx Sun* of the same day, but the most graphic is in the *Mona's Herald* of 2 February 1853:

> *Wednesday the 26th inst. found the town in excitement and bustle. The wind being favourable, about noon the sails were unfurled, the ropes cast off, and amid the cheers of the crowd, and the booming of guns, the gallant* Vixen *glided into the blue water and cleared the old castle in good style. After taking a last farewell of their friends, the schooner got under weigh [sic] and very soon got beyond the range of the spy-glass. She is generally known to be a very fast sailing vessel, and hopes are entertained that she will make the voyage in a short time.*

There are contemporary reports of the voyage, principally in Graves (1968) which includes extracts of the diary of Henry Maddrell Graves. Unfortunately the extracts only cover the first part of the voyage (to 19 March) and the original log has been lost. It seems the voyage took the normal trade route past Madeira and the Cape Verde Islands to the West

Fig 21 The Schooner *Vixen* leaving Peel. Oil on canvas. Unknown artist.

Indies. After picking up the trade winds the route returned east round the Cape of Good Hope and on to Australia. *Vixen* arrived in Melbourne of 3 May 1853, having made the passage of 15,670 statute miles (25,218 km) from Peel in 92 days travelling at a speed of nearly 170 miles (273 km) per day. Much was made of the speed of *Vixen* and the fact that the *Uncle Tom*, a three-masted clipper schooner, had left Douglas the day after *Vixen* but arrived three weeks later. Even the *Prince Arthur*, a fast emigrant ship from Liverpool took two days longer.

Whilst the journey was fast it was not without incident. No sooner had they set off than the first problem was encountered: however well provisioned they were, someone had forgotten to bring any spoons so the adventurers had to whittle some before they could have any soup. Both Captain Cubbon and Thomas Corlett the navigator took ill with fever and had to be carried on deck periodically to take bearings and issue sailing instructions. Several ships were encountered and messages exchanged but, like the spoons, the signalling flags had been left behind, so ships had to be within hailing distance. One encounter could have been disastrous when the American ship *Almeida* on passage from Montevideo to New York mistook them for pirates. H. M. Graves gives a good description of the encounter in his diary:

> *Saturday 5th March*
>
> *Spoke to a ship from Monte Video [sic] to New York by name* Almeida. *We launched our small boat with six men to take letters to the captain who was standing in the gangway. When our boat got alongside the captain would not let the men get on board as he could not understand what all the men were wanted for so small a vessel. He asked our captain how it was that in addition to the six men in the small boat there were 31 on the schooner deck. At this stage the bold* Vixen *was within one mile of his ship. I don't wonder the captain was surprised as the* Vixen *had a two pound shot gun stept in her paul bit on deck at the very time pointed towards his ship. Before we parted we understood each other better and he took our letters and posted them in New York declining money for postage etc.*

Apparently the letters posted in New York arrived in Peel on 27 April. *Vixen* continued her passage to Melbourne and her arrival was noted in the *Melbourne Argus* of 4 May:

> *Arrived –* Vixen, *schooner, 93 tons, T. Cubbon from Isle of Man (January 26th). 37 passengers in intermediate. Captain Cubbon agent.*

Letters posted on arrival reached Peel on the 16 August and thus the *Manx Sun* was able to give a good account of the voyage and arrival when:

> *Many Manx people, recognising the three legs bunting came on board to welcome the first vessel which had arrived from the I.o.M. The company of adventurers were in good health and spirits, and we hope that they may be successful and soon return to their families bringing the little Peel schooner freighted with precious metal.*

The enterprising merchants of Peel were apparently 'animated' by the successful voyage of *Vixen* (*Manx Sun* 19 November 1853). So much so that they decided to send another vessel, the *Peveril*. No doubt they were encouraged by Thomas Gawne's letter (see Appendix 3) stating that 'a fishing luggar might make the passage'. A single masted smack, at 59 tons *Peveril* was much smaller than *Vixen*, but with a proven sailing record. In her six year sailing history prior to 1854, *Peveril* had regularly been part of the winter Mediterranean fruit trade and summer fishing fleet.

After arriving back in Peel on 11 January 1854 with a general cargo from Liverpool, the *Manx Sun* reported that:

> Peveril *has been fitted out, and will take her departure in about a fortnight's time. She is already fully manned, indeed a large number of men applied for berths on board, stimulated most probably by the flattering accounts and tangible remittances which many of the adventurers who went out in* Vixen *have already sent home. The* Peveril *will take out a cargo of Manx manufactured articles, comprising black marble chimney-pieces, and strongly built carts, and also a considerable quantity of red and gray herrings.*

Again in the *Manx Sun* of 25 March:

> *Sailing of another Peel vessel for Australia. The smack* Peveril, *of Peel, Mylechreest, master, sailed yesterday morning. Little more than twelve months have elapsed since we announced the sailing of the schooner* Vixen, *so that this is the second vessel that has been fitted and sent out from Peel. The* Peveril *is a much smaller craft than the* Vixen, *being only 58 tons [sic] register, though her burthen is about 100. Her destination is Melbourne, and she is intended for the coasting and river trade, for which she is said to be well adapted. Her cargo consists of from 20 to 30 tons smiths' slack, a quantity of salt in barrels, 250 barrels and kegs Manx herrings, 500 tin cases red herrings, several tons dried codfish in boxes, 20 carts, and equal number of marble (chiefly Poolvash) chimney-pieces, marble slab tables, a large quantity of spades, ridge tiles, boards, shirts etc. The cargo is the property of the owners of the vessel, Messrs Henry Graves, R. J. Moore, Captain Henry Gill, and others. There are ten persons, including two apprentice lads and two passengers, on board. The value of the vessel and cargo on leaving Peel harbour was estimated at £2,200.*

Fig 22 Moore's Kipper House, Peel (number 13, Fig 2). © Barbara Greenwood

Up until the mid-twentieth century, the Atlantic herring (*Clupea harengus*) was numerous in the Irish Sea. Numbers are drastically reduced today and subject to quota fishing, but in the mid-nineteenth century they were a staple of the Manx diet and preserved by smoking (red herrings) or salting (grey herrings). Both red and grey herrings would have survived the journey to Australia in casks or tins. The word 'kipper' only came into use in the mid-1870s and comes from the Manx *skeddan jiarg*, literally 'red herring'. Manx kippers are still made in Peel in the traditional way by salting and then smoking over oak chips. They are never dyed.

Graves (1968) lists William Cain as one of the adventurers 'From Glen Maye, settled in New Zealand, still living in 1916 aged 92 years'. This may be the William James Cain whose biography appears in the *Cyclopaedia of New Zealand Vol 4* (1905) and who was also part of the crew of *Peveril*. In which case he may have returned from Australia fairly soon after *Vixen's* arrival. See Appendix 5 for Cain's description of *Peveril's* voyage. The following is a summary:

> *William James Cain was one of seven school boys who sailed the cutter* Peveril *from Peel to Melbourne, in the year 1854. The captain of this small band of young adventurers was Thomas Mylechreest. The ship's company consisted of: Thomas Mylechreest (captain) aged 24; John Mylechreest, 22;*

John Cottier, 22; William James Cain, 22; James Moughtin, 19; James Waterson, 19; Phillip Gorry (cook), 16. There was much commotion the day the cutter sailed, and as they were getting ready to sail, the boys' schoolmaster went on board, and said he was proud of them, and felt confident that they were quite competent to do whatever any man could do. He shook hands with all and wished them a good voyage. The adventurers told their friends and families that they would think of them when far away, and promised to write letters with good news for all when they reached Melbourne. The only land the boys sighted on their way out was the Peak of Teneriffe, and then they fell in with the coast of Australia. One day they espied a large ship ahead, the Delaware *of London, bound to Adelaide. The captain of the* Delaware *was very kind, and offered to give the boys anything that they might require; they did not want anything, but asked him to report them when he got to Adelaide; which he did. That was the only tidings that their friends had of them. It was after that that the* Peveril's *troubles began. When they got into the latitude of the Cape, the boys bent a new mainsail, as they expected bad weather, which they got, and had to stow the main and bend a big sail. When the weather moderated the boys set the mainsail, but to their surprise it was rotten in the seams. However, they had good weather then till they reached the coast of Australia, and they made the voyage from Peel to Melbourne in 135 days. Everything considered, the voyage was a memorable one, and is entitled to a place in the annals of navigation.*

Although still young, Thomas Mylchreest was an experienced Master Mariner and had taken *Peveril* on at least one voyage to Iceland. His Master's ticket is dated 24 February 1851 from Tralee (then part of the UK) after seven years apprenticeship.

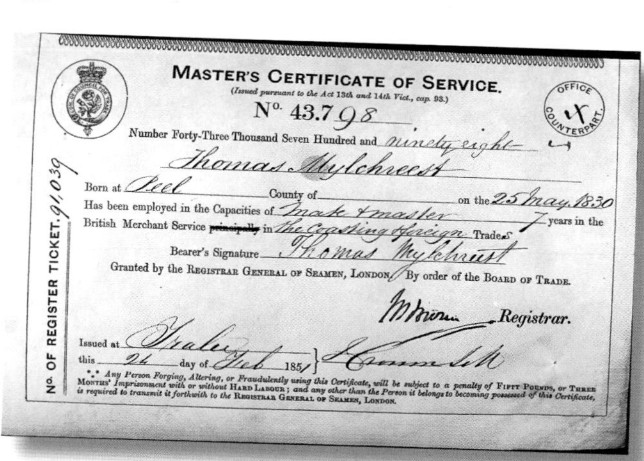

MASTER'S CERTIFICATE OF SERVICE.
(Issued pursuant to the Act 13th and 14th Vict., cap. 93.)
N°. 43.798
OFFICE COUNTERPART.
Number Forty-Three Thousand Seven Hundred and ninety-eight
Thomas Mylchreest
Born at Peel County of ____ on the 25 May 1830
Has been employed in the Capacities of mate & master 7 years in the British Merchant Service ~~principally~~ in the Coasting & foreign Trades
Bearer's Signature Thomas Mylchreest
Granted by the Registrar General of Seamen, London, By order of the Board of Trade.
Registrar.
Issued at Tralee
this 24 day of Feb 1851
*** Any Person Forging, Altering, or Fraudulently using this Certificate, will be subject to a penalty of Fifty Pounds, or Three Months' Imprisonment with or without Hard Labour; and any other than the Person it belongs to becoming possessed of this Certificate, is required to transmit it forthwith to the Registrar General of Seamen, London.
N°. OF REGISTER TICKET. 91,039

Fig 23 Thomas Mylchreest's Master's Ticket. NMM/RSS/M/C/91,039, Thomas Mylchreest Crown Copyright

John Cottier and James Watterson were also ticketed seamen (Cottier number 448310 dated 27 March 1848 and Watterson number 523795 dated 28 May 1851). No doubt the others were also experienced seamen whilst the cook, Philip Gorrey of Strand Lane, Peel was the son of a mariner.

So off they sailed with only the skillful seamanship of Captain Thomas to navigate over 15,000 miles (over 24,000 km) to Melbourne.

Whilst there was an internal telegraph from Melbourne in 1853, there was no underwater cable to link Australia with the rest of the world until 1872. Thus six months later it must have been with great relief that the owners and people of Peel might have noticed a small item in the *Morning Post* (London) of 11 October 1854:

> *SHIP NEWS. Vessels spoken with:* Peveril *(smack), Isle of Man to Melbourne. 36°S, 14°E*

Fig 24 Thomas Mylchreest's Sextant

Fig 25 Thomas Mylchreest's Telescope. Both bequeathed to his brother Joseph (see will, Appendix 10), currently in the Leece Museum, Peel. Photographs: Vic Bates

This sighting was also reported in the Australian papers but erroneously given a passage of eighty days (no doubt misheard or confusion with semaphore). The *Peveril* in fact arrived in Melbourne on 5 August, a passage of four months and twelve days.

The confirmation of safe arrival (rather than an at-sea sighting) would have been when Captain Forbes of the *Lightning* arrived back in Liverpool from Melbourne with shipping intelligence reported in the *Liverpool Mercury* of 23 October. This was followed on 31 October with a more complete entry:

> *The smack* Peveril, *Mylchreest, of Peel, which sailed from that place on the 24th March last, arrived at Melbourne, Australia, on the 5th August, after a run of four months and twelve days, all well.*

This was reported verbatim in the *Manx Sun* of 28 October but also included an extract of a letter sent back from Captain Thomas Mylchreest:

> *The master has written home announcing his arrival there; and stating that freights have fallen greatly. The labour market it would appear, is over stocked, not by the English immigrants but by American and Chinese.*

Peveril's freight was sold and within two weeks she began coastal trading and her career in Australian waters is charted on pages 58 to 72.

Meanwhile *Vixen* had already been in Australian waters for 15 months but the co-operative venture did not have the predicted outcome. There were even rumours of discontent before they reached Melbourne and their agreement appears to have been terminated soon after they arrived. James Lace is credited with acting as peacemaker, as 'with his humorous manner and witty remarks he helped to avoid a mutiny' (Watterson, 1936). *Vixen* and her crew continued coastal trading whilst the adventurers either stayed in Melbourne enjoying a regular wage or split up into small parties to try their luck in the diggings. Apparently they scattered to Ballarat, Bendigo, The Ovens or Mount Alexander.

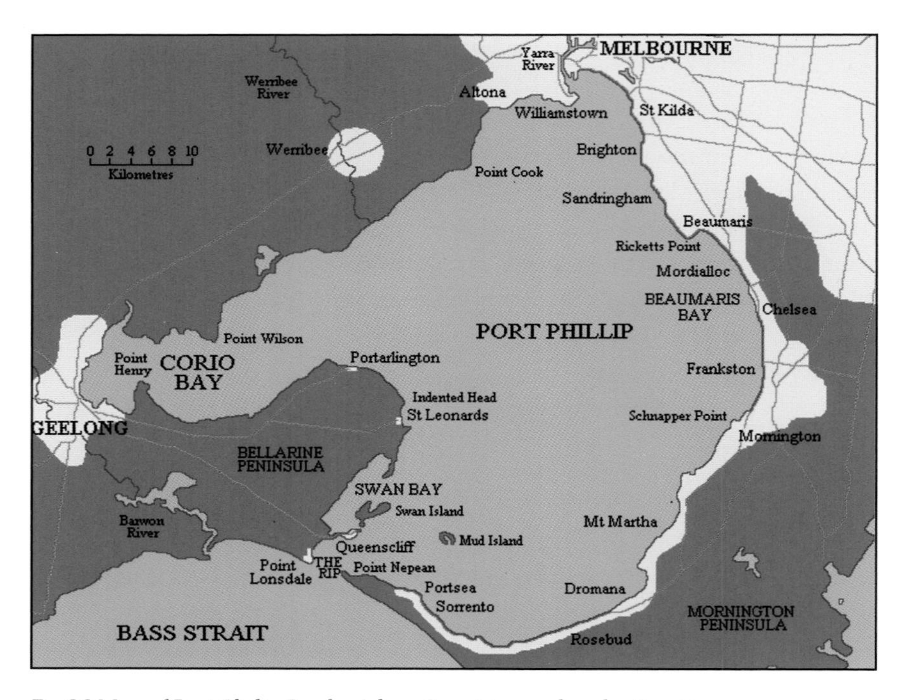

Fig 26 Map of Port Philip Bay by Adam Carr. Licensed under Creative Commons Attribution-Share Alike 3.0 Unported license

Fig 27 Sandridge, Williamstown from Railway Pier. Steel engraving by J. Tingle. Published by Sands and Kenny, 1857. Courtesy of the State Library of Victoria

Fig 28 Modern Melbourne skyline viewed from Hobson's Bay. Wikimedia Commons in the public domain

Vixen's Adventures

ALTHOUGH MELBOURNE HAD yet to reach its goldrush peak, the Manx boys would have found a bustling scene when they tied up at Queen's Wharf in the 'pool' in May 1854 (Fig 29). Williamstown across Hobson's Bay provided another pier and there was plenty of safe anchorage in Port Philip Bay (Figs 27 and 28). By 1856 Melbourne had become the fastest growing and richest port in the British Empire.

Flagstaff Gardens, now a public park, was the place early settlers came for a 'bird's eye view' of the harbour. Signal flags from the flag staff were used to send messages between the harbour and the town. It was probably from here that *Vixen's* arrival was announced.

Vixen, commanded by Captain Thomas Cubbon traded from Melbourne for nearly two years and much of her movement can be tracked through the contemporary newspapers and shipping intelligence. It is not known which of the Manx seamen stayed with her. William James Cain, although listed by Graves (1968), was a doubtful crew member (see page 57). *Vixen's* first voyage after her arrival in Melbourne was one of several to Hobart, Tasmania, across the treacherous Bass Strait (Figs 33 and 34). Transportation of convicts from Britain's overcrowded gaols to Tasmania (Van Diemens Land) had ceased the previous year and Hobart was beginning to establish itself as an important port. Its primary export at

Fig 29 Queen's Wharf, Melbourne, West End. Steel engraving by J. Tingle. Published in *Victoria Illustrated* (1857). Courtesy of the State Library of Victoria

Fig 30 Site of the old Queen's Wharf, River Yarra, Melbourne, 2014.
© Barbara Greenwood

Fig 31 Hobson's Bay &c. from Signal Station. Steel engraving by J. Tingle. Published by Sands and Kenny,1857. Courtesy of the State Library of Victoria

Fig 32 Modern Flagstaff Gardens, Melbourne. © Barbara Greenwood

Fig 33 Hobart Town, Tasmania. Wood engraving by F. Grosse. Published by Enenezer and Syme, 1866. Courtesy of the State Library of Victoria

this time was timber as witnessed by *Vixen's* cargo of October 1853:

30,000ft timber
17,800 shingles
15,175 palings
1870 posts and rails
6 wooden houses

The endemic Tasmanian tree, the Huon Pine (*Lagarostrobus franklinii*) was much prized by shipbuilders and furniture makers. Protected today, reclaimed wood is still much sought after. It was plundered almost to extinction by nineteenth-century loggers and no doubt much of the timber carried by *Vixen* came from this tree. One of the October 1853's journeys from Melbourne was to Hobart and the Huon River further south in order to collect timber.

Vixen's exploits were regularly reported in the Manx press, as this extract from the *Manx Sun* of 11 February 1854 shows:

> *The schooner* Vixen *which sailed in January 1853, and made such a swift voyage, is still doing remarkably well at the Antipodes, where she is employed in the coasting trade – the hands earning some £13 per month.*

In early 1854 *Vixen* made what seems to be an extraordinary voyage. The Hobart *Courier* of 11 January reported *Vixen* outbound to Antipodes Island. Antipodes is part of an inhospitable island group in the subantarctic, some 800 km (nearly 500 miles) E.S.E. of New Zealand's Stewart Island. The main island measures some 7 x 5 km or 7.7 square miles. There are six smaller islands and numerous sea stacks. First discovered by Captain Bligh in 1788, a community of sealers were there in the early nineteenth century but sealing had effectively finished by 1810 after an estimated 330,000 young seals were taken and virtually eliminating the native New Zealand Fur Seal population (Taylor, 2006). Thereafter there was no permanent human population on Antipodes and therefore no reason for *Vixen* to visit. A possible explanation might relate to the renowned navigational skills of Captain Cubbon and other Peel mariners. Antipodes and the nearby Bounty Islands straddled the shortest and quickest course for sailing vessels leaving the Australian gold fields for Europe. However this Southern Great Circle route was very hazardous at the best of times without the presence of poorly charted islands rendered invisible in fog or rough seas. A near correct location of Antipodes at 49°43'S 178°42'E was not established until 1875 and prior to that its

Fig 34 Constitution Dock, Hobart, 2014. © Barbara Greenwood

location had been charted variously over 100 square miles (259 sq. km) of ocean. It is suggested that Captain Cubbon was asked to try and plot an accurate location so that any more ship wrecks could be avoided. For whatever reason, *Vixen* went on to Auckland and returned to Melbourne on 4 March 1854.

Vixen's relatively shallow draught was at an advantage over other vessels and the shipping agents were keen to point this out and that she could sail direct to the wharf without lightering. By June 1854 she had added Sydney to her ports of call, making the passage in well under a week and on one occasion taking only three days.

From the *Empire*, Sydney, 24 June 1854:

> *ONLY VESSEL FOR MELBOURNE DIRECT.*
> *Landing all her Cargo on the Wharf without lightering.*
> *The splendid A1 clipper Schooner* VIXEN, *93 tons register, Thomas Cubbon, commander, is now loading at the Flour Company's Wharf, and having the greater part of her cargo engaged, will have immediate despatch. This Vessel is remarkable for her short passages, and has just made the run from Melbourne in 72 hours.*
> *For Freight only apply to*
> *ANDREW WILSON*
> *474, George-street*

This prompted the agents to advertise:

> *She presents a very desirable opportunity for freight as her late trips from Sydney at the worst season of the year establish her as one of the quickest and safest vessels afloat.*

The Sydney trade appeared to be bringing consumables to Melbourne and the goldfields. Thus her cargo from Sydney in October 1854 included:

70 casks beer
147 cases wine
10 cases cigars
21 packages ironmongery
8 bales drapery
1 hogshead ropes

[hogsheads usually carried liquids, but occasionally other commodities]
5 tierces beef [a tierce was a cask of 42 gallons]
10 tons potatoes

Passengers were also carried as well as freight including a Mr Graves from Sydney to Melbourne in October 1854, but no indication which Mr Graves is involved. A Mr R. Kissack also travelled from Melbourne to Sydney in August 1854. This passage took 12 days in the depths of winter. Geelong and Adelaide were other ports visited and on 13 February 1855 *Vixen* was cleared out from Melbourne for Guichen Bay (167 miles or 270 km south east of Adelaide). This may have been the start of her voyage back to the Isle of Man because the *Manx Sun* reported on 12 May 1855:

> *The* Vixen, *which was navigated out by Mr Corlett, is now on her way home, after having been engaged coasting in the Australian waters for some time with considerable success.*

Fig 35 Map of a portion of South East Australia

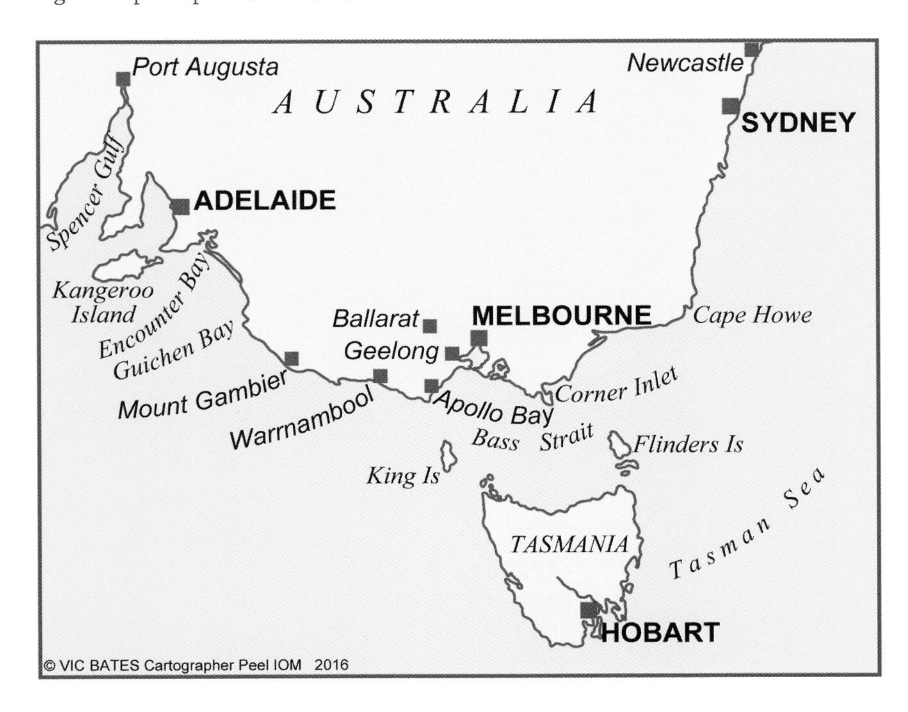

After leaving Guichen Bay *Vixen* appears to have gone to Mauritius where she picked up a cargo of sugar for Liverpool (*Liverpool Mercury*, 6 July 1855). A further stop for more sugar was at St Thomas in the West Indies (Graves, 1968). She was sighted off Cape Clear, County Cork at the beginning of July 1855, and was back in Liverpool soon after. Throughout the remainder of 1855 *Vixen* traded between Liverpool and the Mediterranean having been transferred to the Liverpool Shipping Registry on 4 July 1855. It is not known when she returned to Peel, but it was certainly not trumpeted in the Manx papers in the same way as had her departure. Captain Cubbon relinquished his command in early 1856.

At some stage John Sansbury of Port St Mary became the new Master (Fig 36). It may have been in 1862 which was when he bought eight shares in her from Henry Graves. Up to 1864 *Vixen* continued her coastal voyages before she finally foundered on 26 March 1864. There are conflicting reports of the circumstances of this. A contemporary report (see Appendix 6) says that *Vixen* with Captain Sansbury commanding was on passage from Bordeaux to Belfast and put in to Port St Mary to pick up Mrs Sansbury. About 2.30pm they left Port St Mary and just off the Calf of Man 'a sudden and violent squall caught [*Vixen*] and threw her on

Fig 36 Schooner *Vixen* entering Leghorn [Livorno, Italy] in 1863 under the command of John Sansbury. Oil on canvas. Unknown artist. ©Manx National Heritage

her beam-ends' and she sank immediately. The Castletown lifeboat was despatched but could find no survivors. The Sansburys left three orphan children aged 2, 5 and 7 and it was reported that Henry Graves gave £27 10*s*. to a fund for their benefit. This strongly contrasts with the account given in a lecture by Rev John Quine, Vicar of Lonan and reported in the *Isle of Man Times* of 18 April 1896:

> *One Saturday afternoon she was lying in Peel at the Quay. It was blowing a gale, and the crew were all in the public-house waiting for high water to get out of the harbour. When they came on board they were certainly not in a fit condition to go to sea, and experienced men on the Quay expostulated with them that in the state of the weather they should not go out of the harbour. The skipper of the* Vixen *was reported to have said that if the first port he arrived at should be in the other world, he was going to sail. And so they went out of Peel in the height of the gale. The Peel men went across to the hill, and from the hill watched the* Vixen *until she was lost in the thickness that accompanied a squall, and she was never seen again.*

Fig 37 The Calf Sound, looking towards the Calf of Man from the direction of Cregneash. Wikimedia Commons in the public domain

Whichever version is correct, *Vixen* certainly foundered with all hands. For their bravery the RNLI awarded £1 each to the Castletown lifeboat crew and presented 'Thanks on Vellum' to Henry Corlett Gill on behalf of the crew which that night comprised Wm Callow Cox, Wm Callow Snr., James Callow, Henry Kelly, Richard Kelly, John Callow, John Christian, Wm Caugherty, Thomas Burfoot, Thomas Corlett, and Edw. Hudson. As it was the Castletown rather than Peel lifeboat that was launched, this indicates that the 1864 account is correct and Rev Quine was perhaps issuing a moral lesson, but he was also writing thirty years after the event.

So that was the end of the *Vixen*, but what of the gallant 37 who set off from Peel in 1853 with such high expectations? We know that 14 were married and 23 single and that 14 lived in Peel, 11 in Glen Maye and five in Dalby. Another seven lived elsewhere and included two Cornish miners who had been working in Foxdale. Probably half returned to the Island at some stage, but wherever they dispersed they seem to have kept in contact with one another and the Manx contingent had regular anniversary reunions. By the 35th anniversary in 1888 there were 23 still alive, nine of whom lived on the island. These were Henry Maddrell Graves, John Quayle, Thomas Quilliam, Thomas Radcliffe, John Watterson, Thomas Corlett, Thomas Wattleworth, Thomas Corris and William Watterson. These same nine were still alive at the time of the 39th anniversary, but now out of a total of 15 world wide. The 57th anniversary in 1910 was not marked by the adventurers as only Manxmen Thomas Wattleworth and Thomas Corris were still alive and they were to die within weeks.

The men enjoyed various fortunes of which the following are examples.

Thomas Cubbon gained his Master's ticket in 1850 and captained *Vixen* on both the outward and return voyages. Prior to leaving Peel he had married Margaret Quayle and had three children. After he brought *Vixen* safely back from Australia the family moved to Liverpool where he found employment as a dockgateman and where his son George was born in October 1856. When George was still a baby, the family emigrated to America and Thomas took up farming in Illinois. He paid a visit back to Peel in 1895 and died in Illinois in 1906. George, by then a retired Chief of Police in Wichita, Kansas, visited the Island in 1922.

Thomas Corlett of Dalby was the First Mate and Navigator of *Vixen*. He was the only one of the adventurers who had been to the southern hemisphere before. After he returned to the Island he had a successful career with the Isle of Man Steam Packet Company and was Master successively of *Mona's Isle*, *Mona's Queen* and *Snaefell*.

Jack Gordon was the Second Mate and settled in Australia.

John Cain of Peel settled in Australia and died in Adelaide in 1904.

William Clark(e) returned to Peel and is possibly the father of Ann who married Thomas Mylchreest (see pages 78–82).

William Kermeen from Glen Maye settled in Australia and died in Swanwater, Victoria in 1899.

James Lace returned to the Island but then emigrated to Pennsylvania (Watterson, 1936).

John Quayle and **John Watterson** worked as gold miners in Australia for many years before returning to Peel.

Thomas Wattleworth was well travelled having been to America prior to the *Vixen* voyage. He then went to New Zealand before finally returning to the Island.

Although Graves (1968) states that William Cain 'from Glen Maye, settled in New Zealand, still living in 1916, aged 92', this is more likely to be the William James Cain who was on *Peveril* (see page 42). The *Vixen* William Cain is believed to be the brother of John Cain who died in Melbourne in 1917 (a different John Cain from the above). According to the *Peel City Guardian* of 6 April 1918 he was the last of the *Vixen* men to die and left a bequest to the parish of Patrick, where he was born.

Veronica Kooyman, in her article in the Australian National Maritime Museum's journal *Signals* (volume 103, pages 60–63, 2013), states that a third brother, James, was also with them. If this is the same James, and the family have several manuscripts affirming this, he was one of the first settlers at Natte Yallock, near Avoca in Victoria where his descendants still farm today.

Peveril in Australia

When *Peveril* arrived in Melbourne on 5 August 1854, Captain Thomas Mylchreest's first task would have been to send a letter back to the owners in Peel notifying them of their safe arrival. He then arranged the sale of the cargo through Dansen, Darby & Co. of 59 Flinders Street who placed an advertisement in the *Melbourne Argus* of 9 August 1854:

> *Shipping Intelligence: Imports*
> *August 5 –* Peveril, *from Peel, Isle of Man: 25 tons coal, 14 barrels salt, 24 boxes fish, 88 casks, 172 kegs, 478 tins herring, 20 carts, 20 chimneypieces, 4 washstands, 2 dozen spades, 70 tiles, 43 dozen shirts, Dansen, Darby & Co.*

Presumably the marble chimney pieces and washstands were intended for the new settlement whilst the spades, carts etc. were destined for the goldfields.

Less than two weeks after the end of their intrepid voyage, *Peveril's* crew began coastal trading, leaving Melbourne for Geelong on 18 August. Their next voyage was a round trip to Sydney, followed by other local trips (Fig 35).

At the beginning of 1855 Captain Thomas had changed agent to Ewart & Ginn of 93 Flinders Street, but continued trading with Geelong etc. A direct trip to Adelaide was advertised at the end of February (arrived 7 March) and returned to Melbourne via Portland. Ewart & Ginn had a regular packet service between Melbourne and Sydney, and the *Peveril* joined this for much of the rest of the year, presumably carrying general cargo. A sad interlude was reported in the *Melbourne Argus* of 6 September 1855:

> *One pound reward – lost from cutter* Peveril, *lying at the Gas Company's wharf, small black Scotch terrier dog, short-legged, white breast, with a brass collar.*

It is not known if the dog was recovered.

More coastal trading occurred during 1856 but also at least two trips to Auckland, New Zealand, a journey of up to a month across the Tasman Sea which included the import of 35,000 feet of timber from Auckland in October 1856.

Sometime towards the end of 1855, Captain Thomas applied to the owners in Peel for permission to sell *Peveril*. The certificate of sale was drawn up dated 20 May 1856, sent to Melbourne, and the sale put in the hands of Beaver & Coffey who advertised the sale in the *Melbourne Argus*:

> *TUESDAY, 31st DECEMBER*
> *Clipper Cutter* Peverill.
> *Built at the Isle of Man.*
> *H. A. COFFEY, of Beaver and Coffey, will sell by auction, at their rooms 36 Collins Street West, on Tuesday, 31st inst., at eleven o'clock,*
> *The Clipper Cutter*
> PEVERILL,
> *59 tons register, 100 tons burthen, coppered and copper fastened, and in first rate sea going condition.*
> *This beautiful little vessel was built in the Isle of Man, of the best English oak, and classed in Liverpool in the year 1848, and thoroughly overhauled and sheathed with Muntz heavy metal just prior to her leaving England in the year 1854.*
> *Her outfit, including sails, masts, rigging, anchors, chains, boat gear, are all in first rate condition, and of the best material. Her sailing qualities are of the first order, and from her light draft of water (9 feet with 100 tons dead weight) she is, perhaps, one of the most desirable vessels that have been offered in this market for a long time.*
> *Terms at Sale*

Presumably the sale went ahead as advertised on 31 December 1856 but may have been re-sold because the Melbourne registry states:

> *The cutter* Peveril *formerly of Peel, Isle of Man registered anew in consequence of a sale dated the 25th day of March 1857. Made by Thos. Mylchreest, attorney for Hy. Graves and others, owners under a certificate of sale dated the 15th May 1856.*

Peveril was bought by Arthur Devlin who provided his own crew. Although this was effectively the end of the Manx connection, apart from a short interlude in 1873/75 (see pages 68–69), *Peveril* continued to trade in Australian waters for a further eventful 28 years. The crew dispersed and their later history is given on pages 73 to 82.

Captain Arthur Devlin (1810–93) was a prominent Melbourne merchant and a founding member of the Melbourne Athenaeum Club (Fig 38). He was the son of an Irish activist who had been transported to Australia in 1800. Arthur was born in 1810 and went to sea at the age of 12 and amassed a small fortune in the whaling trade. He owned and traded many ships including the *Surprise,* Australia's first steamship. Along the way he survived 40 days shipwrecked after his brig *Rapid* struck the Conway Reef near Fiji in 1840. He lived in Melbourne

Fig 38 Captain Arthur Devlin Photograph, Johnstone, O'Shannessy & Co. In collection: City of Melbourne Jubilee of the Incorporation of the City, 1892. Courtesy of the State Library of Victoria

Fig 39 Villa in East Melbourne, 2014 Similar to one where Captain Devlin lived © Barbara Greenwood

and built a handsome villa at 124 Wellington Parade (demolished in 1967 and now the site of the East Melbourne Post Office, Fig 39). *Peveril* joined his fleet in 1857.

More coastal voyages continued under the new ownership, mostly within a few days' sailing of Melbourne. The growing town had a huge demand for timber and *Peveril* brought timber and sleepers in from such places as Apollo Bay and Corner Inlet. The rapid influx of people was more than the town could house or care for. In just four months in 1852, 619 ships arrived in Hobson's Bay carrying 55,057 immigrants. Prior to permanent dwellings, Melbourne had a series of vast tented villages (Fig 11). Admittedly many of the men went straight to the diggings and at times the town was populated by wives and children. Many of them drifted back or, not finding their fortunes in gold, decided to make a living in the service industries.

Fig 40 Port of Warrnambool. Steel engraving by J.Tingle. Published in *Victoria Illustrated* (1857). Courtesy of the State Library of Victoria

Fig 41 The Warrnambool Potato Harvest (digging and bagging potatoes). Wood engraving. Published in *Illustrated Australian News* 12 March 1881. Courtesy of the State Library of Victoria

Fig 42 The Warrnambool Potato Harvest (loading lighters). Wood engraving. Published in *Illustrated Australian News* 12 March 1881. Courtesy of the State Library of Victoria

During 1857 *Peveril* made regular journeys to Warrnambool, initially when it was an important port for the goldfields but later for the export of potatoes. Food supplies in Melbourne were seriously threatened by the growing population and the fertile agricultural land around Warrnambool provided a range of foods but particularly potatoes (Figs 40, 41 and 42).

By 1858 *Peveril* had been sold to Thomas George Chapman (*c.* 1835–94), a Master Mariner and successful owner of several schooners. The new Master was Captain Robert Poat. An interesting article appeared in the *Warrnambool Examiner* in March 1858:

> *We understand Captain Chapman, the owner of the* Peveril, *is about purchasing another fine vessel for this trade. The coasters materially interfere with the* Lady Bird *in their trips from this [port] to Melbourne, taking generally a good compliment of passengers. If favourable winds could be depended on (especially in the passage from Melbourne) we feel convinced there would be very little for the* Lady Bird *to do as far as Warrnambool is concerned, in consequence of the exorbitant charges both for passengers and freight, and the general want of attention to the interests of the port.*

The *Lady Bird* was a clipper-bowed steamship of 420 tons built in Dumbarton, Scotland in 1851 and had regular schedules out of Melbourne to Warrnambool and then Hobart, Tasmania. It is amazing to think that a single-masted sailing smack could compete on this passage with a steam ship seven times her size.

Captain Chapman was obviously well-respected and gave evidence to the Warrnambool Council on improvements needed to the harbour in 1867. This might well have been as a result of his experiences in 1863/64 which nearly saw the end of *Peveril*. The night of 5/6 July 1863 was particularly stormy in Warrnambool and brought about the foundering of *Peveril* and total loss of the *Golden Spring*.

From *The Age*, Melbourne Friday 10 July 1863 (further reports are given in Appendix 7):

> *One of the most terrific gales we have ever witnessed in this port took place yesterday, and has resulted in the total loss of one vessel and the stranding of another. The sloop* Peveril, *that well-known*

> *and favourite Warrnambool trader, was nearly high and dry broadside on to the beach.*

Peveril's perishable cargo of salt, sugar etc. was lost but on closer examination by Captain Chapman when he arrived from Melbourne, it appeared that the ship was not seriously damaged. However she was stuck fast on the shore and it wasn't until seven months later in February 1864 that she was finally refloated and limped back to Melbourne.

From the *Warrnambool Advertiser*, 23 February 1864:

> *The* Peveril *– We have much pleasure in stating that during a high tide on Friday evening last, this favorite trader was floated off safely, and is now at her old anchorage. We are happy to state also that she is perfectly watertight and sound, and will very shortly take her departure for Melbourne. If ever a man deserves the thanks of the community, Captain Chapman does, for his unwearied perseverance in sticking for seven months to the* Peveril, *until he did get her off.*

Repairs were obviously necessary and an advert appeared in the *Melbourne Argus* of 7 March 1864:

> *Wanted, two joiners, fit up cabin etc. Apply on board cutter,* Peveril, *South-bank, near Falls.*

By 12 March she was re-registered with the Melbourne registry because of the tonnage alterations, the new tonnage figure being 58.64 tons. At the end of the month she was ready to commence trading again (*Melbourne Argus*, 28 March):

> *For Warrnambool – the cutter* Peveril, *having undergone a thorough overhaul and refit, will receive cargo on Tuesday and Wednesday next at the Australian Wharf.*

The Warrnambool trading continued throughout the 1860s but by the end of the decade the Victorian goldrush had all but finished, although gold continues to be found there to this day.

Captain Chapman thought to realise his asset and put *Peveril* up for sale in 1871:

From the *Melbourne Argus, 11 August 1871:*

Sales by Auction

TUESDAY, AUGUST 22.

PEVERIL *CUTTER.*

To Those Engaged in the South Sea Islands, Fiji, Pearl Fishery, and other Trades generally, requiring the services of a first-class British-built cutter.

H. A. Coffey has received instructions to SELL by AUCTION, on Tuesday, 22nd August, at the Melbourne Shipping Exchange, Collins-street west, at twelve noon,

The Peveril *cutter.*

This vessel is now in the market for sale, having been long and favourably known in the Western trade from this port to Warrnambool. It is an established fact that she has carried her cargoes as reliably and with very nearly the regularity of the steamers engaged in the same trade. She is 59 tons register, carries 100 tons general cargo, is now in first-class order, has been metalled 18 months since and has undergone a thorough refit to masts, sails and rigging Her dimensions are – Length 57ft, breadth 19ft, depth 10ft. Inventories at the rooms of the auctioneer.

Chapman obviously changed his mind about selling *Peveril* and in September 1871 engaged Captain Booth to take her to Fiji with cargo for Levuka, Suva and Tavuini. A passage of over 2,000 miles (nearly 4,000 km) would have been easy in comparison to the passage from Peel to Melbourne. Unfortunately nothing is known about the voyage, other than the press advertisement for cargo, but *Peveril* was back in Australian waters by mid-1872. She was transferred to the Sydney shipping register on 26 February 1873, and Captain Chapman was back in command. By this time pearls were becoming the new gold in Australia and Chapman decided to take *Peveril* to the Torres Strait off the Cape York peninsula in Far North Queensland. Pearling had begun here in 1868 where *Beche-de-Mer* (sea cucumber) fisheries were already established using indigenous divers. Pearling used schooners such as *Peveril* as mother ships with six to eight associated luggers each crewed by islanders. European divers using breathing apparatus were appearing by 1874, but prior to that all diving was by indigenous people. By 1877, 109 vessels (including 63 with divers using breathing apparatus) were working in the Torres Strait from either Somerset on Cape York or Thursday Island (Pixley, 1971). A graphic account of pearl fishing in 1875 in the Torres Strait is given in a letter from Mr J. Small, a diver from England who was employed on *Peveril* (see Appendix 8).

The search was for gold-lipped pearls (*Pinctada maxima*) and black-lipped pearls (*P. margarifera*) with the shells being brought to the surface and transferred to the mother ship daily. Only then would the shells be opened, because although the main market was the shell itself for mother-of-pearl, used extensively to make buttons and jewellery, it was a real prize and bonus if there was a pearl inside. Obviously the schooner captain wanted to supervise this himself. Pearling still operates in the Torres Strait today but is strictly controlled by the size of shell collected and only hand methods can be used.

The 1870s were a very profitable period for pearl fishing and the cargo from one voyage was sold at auction as advertised in the *Sydney Morning Herald* of 10 December 1872:

Finest Torres Straits
Pearl Shell
Just arrived ex Peveril
FROM BOOBY ISLAND
R F Stubbs and Co will sell by auction at the Rooms,
this day at a quarter to 1 sharp.
Portion of the cargo of the
FINEST PEARL SHELL
Ever imported into this market
Full particulars of which will be given at sale
In lots to suit buyers
Terms cash

This had obviously been a very successful voyage and the following article appeared in the *Rockhampton Journal* in January 1873:

> *Some time ago Captain Chapman left Melbourne in the cutter* Peveril *on a pearl fishing cruise. He has shown the people of Queensland how to make money. The schooner was out six months on a pearl fishing cruise, and has lately returned to Sydney with ninety tons of shell. This has just been sold at auction, and realised, we are informed, a gross of £16,000. The expenses of the cruise are comparatively trifling so that nearly the whole amount is profit. This pearl fishing pays, we should think, better than quartz reefing or mining, and is far safer, as well as more profitable than kidnapping Polynesians.*

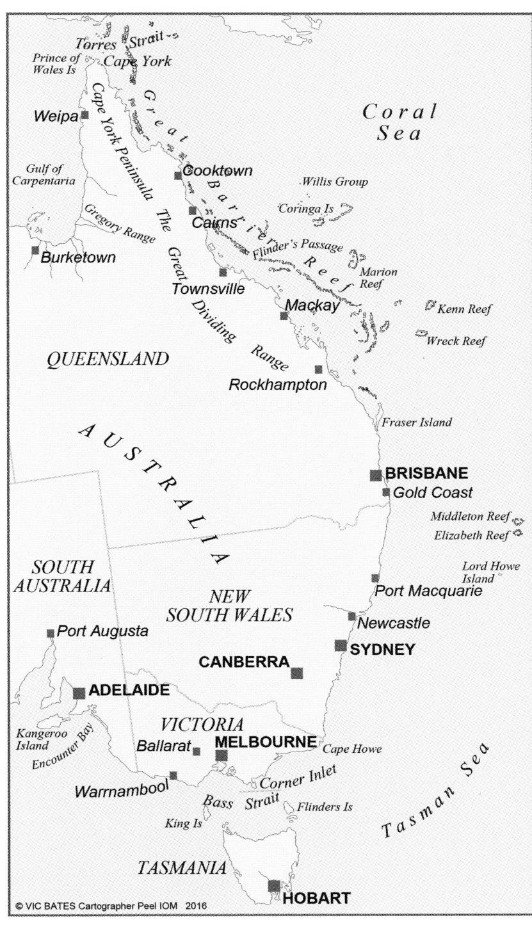

Fig 43 Map of the East Coast of Australia

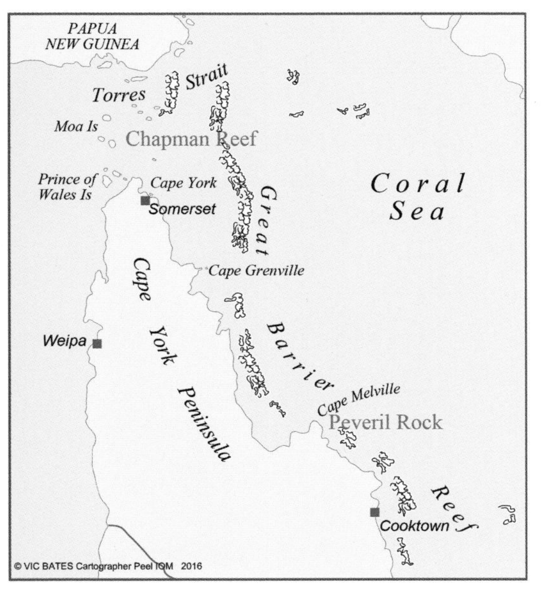

Fig 43A Map of Far North Queensland showing Peveril Rock and Chapman Reef

The reference to kidnapping Polynesians related to the practice of 'Blackbirding' which was fairly common at the time. People from Vanuatu, Papua New Guinea and the Solomon Islands in particular were taken to work in the Queensland sugar cane plantations. Officially they were known as 'indentured labourers' but the practice was highly controversial and they were effectively slaves, known colloquially as Kanakas (Docker, 1981). There is no evidence to suggest that *Peveril* was part of this trade.

Captain Chapman was obviously a skilled navigator, and on this 1872 voyage he was able to chart various parts of the reef that were hazards to shipping. Thus he gave an accurate location of a dangerous reef, subsequently known as Chapman Reef, between Wednesday and Horn islands in the Torres Strait (Fig 43A). He also charted a dangerous coral patch which he named Peveril Rock on the inner reef passage between Barrow and Noble islands. Although successful it doesn't appear that Chapman made any further voyages on *Peveril* to the Torres Strait but he is recorded as making voyages in other ships such as *the John S Lane* in 1875.

In February 1873 *Peveril* was re-united with Captain John Mylchreest. Captain John had been part of the original crew, under the command of

Fig 44 Cooktown, Queensland, from the north shore. Wood engraving. Published by David Syme & Co in *Illustrated Australian News*, 1879.
Courtesy of the State Library of Victoria

his brother Thomas, who sailed from Peel nearly 20 years earlier. For the next two years Captain John traded with *Peveril* from Sydney along the coast of New South Wales and Queensland as far north as Townsville, primarily with sugar and timber. Eventually she was sold in Sydney to Alfred Lamb on 15 March 1875, and subsequently to Charles Parbury on 30 September 1879. Lamb and Parbury was an important Sydney shipping and merchant company founded by Alfred's father John Lamb and Charles' father Frederick Parbury. The company split to become Alfred Lamb & Co, and Parbury, Henty & Co but the two men continued as business associates and *Peveril* was traded between them. Alfred Lamb pioneered the export of frozen meat and was elected to the New South Wales Legislative Assembly and was still a member at the time of his early death in 1890 aged 45. Charles Parbury moved to London in 1880 but still maintained his considerable Australian business interest until his death in London in 1915. He was a keen sailor and a founder member of the Royal Sydney Yacht Squadron in 1862.

Throughout the remainder of the 1870s *Peveril* continued to trade along the New South Wales and Queensland coasts based in Sydney. She was sold on 20 December 1879 to Frederick Joshua Wathen Beardmore of Cooktown, Queensland. Cooktown was having its own goldrush in the 1870s after gold was found in the Palmer River in 1872 and the town developed as the servicing port at the mouth of the Endeavour River. By 1880 there may have been as many as 7,000 people in the area. Beardmore, a Commission Agent, was one of the early merchants of Cooktown and was well respected. *Peveril* was added to his fleet to service the booming township and also returned to the Torres Strait where she had been pearling with Captain Chapman ten years earlier. To the pearl fishing voyages were added trips to fish for *Beche-de-Mer* (sea cucumber) which is considered a delicacy in East and South-east Asian cookery. It is still fished today but numbers are strictly controlled, as with pearl fishing, and limited to free-diving with hand tools only. There was no such restriction in 1881 when the *Cooktown Herald* reported:

> *Beche-de-Mer. Notwithstanding the unfavourable weather, some of the fishermen have been unusually fortunate, the* Peveril *for instance having sent in 6½ tons, the result of only a few weeks fishing. Mr Beardmore has now seventeen tons on hand.*

Perhaps dried and exported, it was more likely sold to the numerous Chinese who flocked to the goldfields around Cooktown.

On the 21 February 1884 Cooktown experienced a severe storm which had dreadful consequences on the town and harbour. Although not officially called a cyclone, it must have been linked to one that unroofed the whole of Bowen township and caused heavy flooding in Mackay, south

Fig 45 Sandbanks off the bathing pool, Cooktown Photograph courtesy of the Cooktown History Centre.

Fig 46 The Endeavour River, Cooktown from Grassy Hill Lookout, 2015 © Barbara Greenwood

Fig 47 Modern Cooktown, 2015. © Barbara Greenwood

of Cairns. The *Maryborough Chronicle* of 22 February published the initial account:

> *Terrible weather has been experienced at Cooktown. Twenty four inches of rain fell in twenty four hours, accompanied by a strong gale. The schooners Prompt, 86 tons, and* Peveril, *59 tons, drifted on to the bar.*

A full and graphic account is given in the *Cairns Post* of 28 February 1884 (see Appendix 9). *Peveril* drifted onto sandbanks 'almost opposite the bathing shed'. The bathing shed and pool were later destroyed in the 1907 cyclone. Thus the photograph (Fig 45) must pre-date 1907 and clearly shows the treacherous nature of the sandbanks at the mouth of the Endeavour River at Cooktown.

There is a tantalising note from a Port Douglas 'correspondent' in the *Queenslander* of 6 September 1884:

> *Port Douglas August 22:*
> *The cutter* Peveril, *from New Guinea, called in here during the week on her way to Cooktown. Among her crew were some New Guinea natives, and we were treated to the sight of a chief of that place in "full feathers".*

However the 'correspondent' most likely got the name of the ship mixed up because it is clear that *Peveril* did indeed founder in the gale six months earlier. Peter Stone (2006) states that *Peveril* was destroyed by a gale that battered Cooktown on 21 February 1884. The minute book of the Maritime Board of Queensland (Queensland State Archives item ID71600, minutes dated 26 March 1884) confirms this when

> *A report of an enquiry into the loss of* Peveril *at Cooktown was read.*

Unfortunately the original report no longer exists. The final closure is given in the Sydney Shipping Register:

> *Went ashore on the sand spit inside Endeavour River bar, Queensland, sometime early in 1884, about February. Was declared a wreck, and burnt for her copper. Register closed 11th day of May 1885.*

Peveril's last owner, F. J. W. Beardmore, died on 21 November 1884 'with somewhat unexpected suddenness at the age of 41 years' [Epilepsy] (*Queensland Figaro* 6 December 1884). He died intestate and Letters of Administration were granted to his widow, Emily Ann, who administered all his lands, goods, chattels, credits and effects, which presumably included the wreck of *Peveril*. It was probably she or her Managing Clerk, Bob Houston, who decided that there was no future in refloating *Peveril*, so she was burned for her copper.

So ended this gallant Peel sailing ship, but her memory lives on in the lives and descendants of those who owned her and sailed in her (see next two Chapters).

The Next Generation

SO, WHAT HAPPENED to the original *Peveril* crew? After she was sold in 1856, it is thought that they found their way to the Victorian goldfields to try their hand at mining and no doubt met up with some of the *Vixen* men.

Thomas and John Mylchreest may have gone on to Gympie, Queensland which was having its own goldrush. However both appeared to be singularly unsuccessful and the brothers separated at that point. John went to Maryborough, Queensland where he worked in the timber business but the lure of the sea was still strong and he bought the 34 ton schooner *Mona* which he traded along the Queensland and New South Wales coasts. As stated on page 68 he was briefly reunited with *Peveril* and whilst he was working her, *Mona* was lost:

Maryborough Chronicle, Wide Bay and Burnett Advertiser, Saturday 17 April 1875:

> *Advice was received in town yesterday of the total wreck of the schooner* Mona *at No 6 island of the Percy Group. She was owned by Captain Mylchreest, of Maryborough, and commanded by Captain Westray. She left this port about February last, for Mackay, she reached her destination safely, and has since been trading in the North. She was insured in the New Zealand and Pacific Insurance Offices for £200 with each. The telegram was received from Gladstone, and as there is no mention of any lives being lost, we presume that the crew made that port in safety.*

John's next command was the *John S Lane*, an 82 ton schooner which primarily traded Queensland sugar, and which Captain Chapman also appeared to have captained at one stage. Whilst in Maryborough he married Annie Loague, sister of William Loague, a Brisbane baker. William and Annie were two of the children of Robert Loague and Annie (née Adair) an Irish immigrant family who had arrived in Brisbane aboard the *Fiery Star* in 1863. John and Annie Mylchreest had three children, Christina Annie (Chrissie), Elizabeth and John Adair. Annie was living at the family home in Ann Street, Fortitude Valley, Brisbane when she died suddenly of a brain haemorrhage on 17 February 1876. This change in circumstances and the care of three small children, coupled with John's appointment as the first Government Pilot of Cairns, Queensland led him to finally end his coastal sailing career. John knew the reef coast well and was an ideal choice as the first Gazetted Pilot of the new port of Trinity Bay (Cairns) on 21 October 1876. The Queensland pilot service had only

Fig 48 Anchor marking the site of the first official landing party at Cairns, 6 October 1876 (taken in 2015) © Barbara Greenwood

been founded four years earlier. He arrived on the *Porpoise* with other government officials to pitch their tents opposite the site of the future Strand Hotel on the Esplanade and administer the new township (Fig 48).

John was well liked in Cairns, and to quote a memoire published in the *Peel City Guardian* of 30 April 1910:

> *Captain John Mylchreest was a handsome man of fine presence, weighing over 17 stones. The Captains of vessels find in him a very kind friend who would go out of his way to serve them. He was a very kindly, but still a very firm and strict man. Captain Fowles (Marine Superintendent of the Harbour Board of Cairns) who was a great friend of Captain Mylchreest's says of him that he was the most sincere man he ever knew. He called a spade a spade. He was good-hearted and where he was a friend there was no shaking his friendship. Captain Fowles who was at Melbourne at the time of the arrival of the* Peveril *says the long voyage of so small a craft was the talk of the place. The navigation of Captain Thomas Mylchreest her skipper was highly commended, and the pluck and daring of her crew greatly praised.*

During his time in Cairns, John amassed a large collection of shells and aboriginal artefacts which, according to Jones (1976) were bought by Robert Logan Jack (1845–1921) who for many years was the Government Geologist for Queensland. Jack's collection is now in the Queensland Museum, but contains no Mylchreest specimens. However in John's will dated 4 November 1888, he leaves the 'collection of shells in my house' to his daughter Chrissie. The whereabouts of his collection must therefore remain unknown. He left his cottage and butcher's shop on Lake Street, Cairns to Chrissie and the rest of his estate to his son John Adair. His daughter Elizabeth had died young and John Adair died in Cairns in 1896 aged 25. Nothing more is known about him, but he never married, so the Mylchreest name has not carried on through him, although there are other Mylchreests in Australia.

Captain John developed cancer and went to Melbourne for treatment, but he died on 8 November 1888 aged 56. According to his death certificate he died of 'sloughing of tumour of the face' but the memoire published in the *Peel City Guardian* of 30 April 1910 (above) has a non-medical explanation:

It appears that when a boy at sea he received a heavy blow from a block, which always in after life affected him to some extent, and this no doubt was the root of the disease [cancer].

There are no surviving photographs of John to support this. He died at 492 Lygon St, Carlton, Melbourne and is buried in Melbourne General Cemetery (Figs 49 and 50). His obituary was published in the *Cairns Post* of 14 November 1888:

The late Pilot Mylchreest.
The death of Pilot Mylchreest removes one more of the old Cairns pioneers. The stout old mariner has sailed out upon the ocean of Eternity, and never more will look upon the terrestrial seas from the deck of the white-winged ship.

His soul has sight of that immortal sea
Which brought us hither;
He sees the children sport upon the shore
And hears the mighty waters rolling evermore.

In years gone by the old man was captain of the coasting schooner "John S. Lane," *and the cutter* Peveril, *trading from Brisbane to the Northern ports. He was appointed pilot at Cairns about the end of 1876, and has remained here ever since. Before he arrived he had lost his wife, who died in in Brisbane, bequeathing him three children, one of whom a little girl, he lost in Cairns, leaving only one son, now about sixteen years of age, and one daughter, the respected wife of our respected citizen, H.M.Simmonds J.P. He had a brother, a very fortunate and wealthy miner on the South African diamond fields. The old man's death removes a face and form long familiar to Cairns.*

Chrissie was John's sole surviving child and kept house for him until her marriage to Henry Simmonds in 1884. Sugar cane is the principal crop of the Cairns area of Queensland, and in 1882 Chrissie was invited to put the first cane through the rollers of the Hop Wah Pioneer Sugar Mill. Chrissie and Henry lived for some time in the Lake Street house in Cairns, but then set up home at Highleigh, Gordonvale, south of Cairns. The Mulgrave Central Sugar Mill in Gordonvale was constructed in 1895 and Henry became its Chairman. The mill exists to this day, now under the ownership of MSF Sugar.

Fig 49 Burial plot (no headstone) of John Mylchreest in Melbourne General Cemetery, 2015. © Barbara Greenwood

Fig 50 House on Lygon Street, Melbourne, built in 1886. Contemporary with and opposite the one where John Mylchreest died in 1888. © Barbara Greenwood

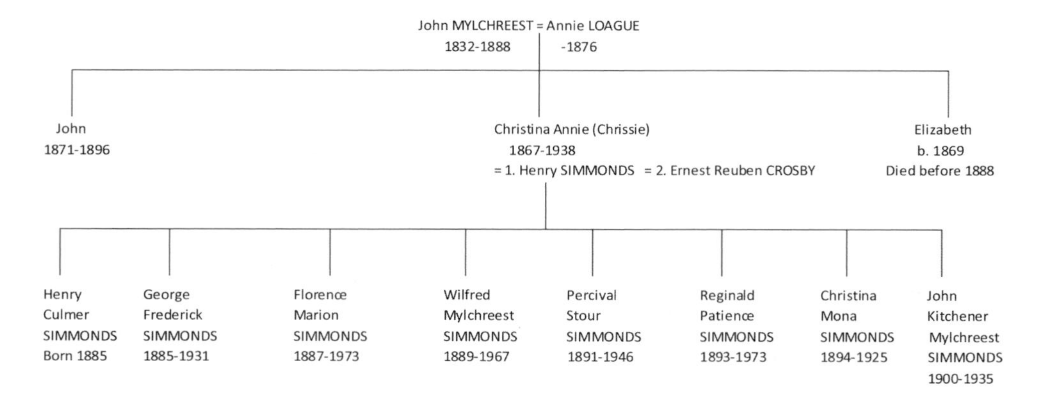

Fig 51 Simplified tree of the descendants of John Mylchreest (1832–88)

Henry and Chrissie had eight children whose numerous descendants still live in Australia (see Fig 51). After Henry's death in 1900, Chrissie married Ernest Reuben Crosby. She died in Babinda, Queensland in 1938 aged 72.

There is a surviving letter (copy in Mylchreest family archives) which indicates that Chrissie paid a visit to the Isle of Man. It is undated but appears to have been written in the 1920s. In it she states: 'I thought it [the Isle of Man] the loveliest spot I had ever known. I was taken to Peel and shown the very house where my Grandfather Mylchreest lived and where my father and all his brothers and sisters were born and reared.'

Four of the Simmonds boys served in the First World War. Two of them, Reginald Patience Simmonds and Wilfred Mylchreest Simmonds served in France where Reginald lost a leg. Whilst he was convalescing and they were both awaiting repatriation to Australia, they visited the Isle of Man. There is a photograph (Fig 53) of them with other family members, including the author's mother, Kathleen as a young child, outside the Whitehouse, Kirk Michael.

Thomas Mylchreest returned to the Isle of Man from Melbourne in July 1870 on the clipper ship *Suffolk* and was back in Peel at the time of the 1871 census which shows he was living with his younger brother Robert at 2, Queen Street, Peel. Robert had married Sage Quayle in 1868 and their daughter Edith May was just a baby at the time. Shortly afterwards Robert and his young family emigrated to Cleveland, Ohio, but on census night 1871 they were all living in Queen Street with William Gawne and

Fig 52 Chrissie Simmonds (née Mylchreest) with her children in 1908.
Back row: Wilfred Mylchreest, George Frederick (Fred), Percival Stour (Percy), Henry Culmer (Harry), Reginald Patience
Front row: John Kitchener Mylchreest (Jack), Florence Marion (Florrie), Chrissie, Christina Mona. Simmonds family archive

Fig 53 Whitehouse, Kirk Michael, 1919. Back row (left to right) Reginald Patience Simmonds, Joseph S. Mylchreest, Ada Mylchreest, Doris Lister (sister of Ethel Mylchreest), Wilfred Mylchreest Simmonds. Front row (left to right) Ethel Mylchreest, Brian Mylchreest, Phoebe Hannah Mylchreest (widow of Joseph Mylchreest), Tommy Mylchreest, Kathleen Mylchreest. Mylchreest family archives

Fig 54 Grave of Thomas Mylchreest, Peel New Cemetery. © Barbara Greenwood

James Reed as lodgers. Of interest is the presence of the young servant girl, Jemima Mylchreest aged 13. Jemima is the daughter of their brother Joseph Mylchreest and his first wife Catherine Skelly who had died very shortly after giving birth and who was brought up by various family members whilst her father was seeking his fame and fortune around the world. A simplified tree of the Mylchreests of Peel can been seen on page 17 (Fig 4).

It is likely that Thomas knew Ann Clark before he set sail to Australia (she would have been 19 when *Peveril* sailed). However they renewed their acquaintance on Thomas' return to Peel and were married soon after. Ann was the daughter of William Clark (1807–48) a baker and licensee of the Peveril public house in Peel and his wife Margaret née Leece (1803–53).

He may have been the same William Clark who was one of the *Vixen* adventurers. Among their other children were Eliza Margaret (1843–1932) and Angus (1845–1919).

On his return to Peel, Thomas took command of the *Manx Minx* (registered number 27256) which was a 2-masted schooner of 78 tons. She had been built in Henry Graves' yard in 1860 and Graves was the managing owner. *Manx Minx's* voyages during the two years Thomas was Master included trips to the Mediterranean (Bari in Italy and Prevesa in Greece) and the Azores.

Thomas' last command was the *Western Maid* (registered number 49800), another Graves' built 2-masted schooner but at 147 tons was about double the size of *Manx Minx*. As a consequence in the four years Thomas was Master, he was able to take her on longer voyages as well as the regular Mediterranean fruit trade. An example of this is the journey of 4,600 miles (7,402 km) to St Helena in 1875. St Helena in the south Atlantic is one of the world's most remote islands but was an important stop over for ships travelling from Europe to Asia and South Africa and then as now, required regular shipped supplies. This has now changed with the opening of the Island's first airport, landing at which is not without its hazards due to extreme wind shear. The first commercial flight to St Helena took place on 20 May 2016.

Fig 55 Grave of Thomas Mylchreest (detail).
© Barbara Greenwood

Western Maid's return trip from St Helena was via Bahia, Brazil. She made several journeys to St John's, Newfoundland, a distance of over 2,300 miles (3,700 km) across the north Atlantic. Thomas' last voyage with *Western Maid* was a Newfoundland one in 1877 with sailing orders:

> *'Voyage: Glasgow to Gibraltar, Cadiz, then to Newfoundland and/ or Labrador, thence to the Mediterranean to and from, as may be required until the ship returns to a final port of discharge in the United Kingdom, with liberty to call at port for orders. Probable period of engagement – 12 months. The crew on board to be sober at all times stated or the Master may ship others in their place. No spirits allowed. Signed Thomas Mylchreest, 15 May 1877.'*

The voyage terminated in Hove on 2 January 1878.

Thomas continued coastal sailing before retiring to Peel where he had a grocer's shop and served as a Peel Town Commissioner. His spirit of adventure was not quite extinguished as he made a trip to South Africa and managed some of Joseph's diamond mines in Griqualand West. Finally returning in 1888 he purchased Glenaspet in Patrick where he died in 1892 aged 62. He is buried in Peel new churchyard along with his wife who died in 1896. They are in the same plot as Thomas' mother Christian Mylchreest who had died in 1867. Interestingly the headstone inscription has space for his father John but this is left blank because he died off Cork and has no known grave.

Thomas' will is dated 5 March 1890 (see transcript Appendix 10). Apart from the bequests to various Mylchreest family members, Angus Clark is Ann's brother and her sister is Eliza Jones.

Details of the remaining five *Peveril* men are sketchy apart from those of William James Cain who emigrated to New Zealand. His fascinating story of *Peveril's* passage to Australia is given in Appendix 5. James Watterson ended up in South Africa although he did pay one visit back to Peel in 1897. John Cottier remained at sea and appears to have died a bachelor. His sisters, Christian and Sarah were respected ladies outfitters in Douglas who retired in 1897, selling their business to T. H. Cowin. Nothing more is known of James Moughtin or Philip Gorry.

Conclusion

ALTHOUGH IT IS over 160 years since *Vixen* and *Peveril* sailed from Peel on their adventures, memories live on in the people and places of both the Isle of Man and Australia. Even though seafaring was in the blood of both crews, and long sea journeys were considered normal for many Manxmen, that they all survived the perils of the journey in such small vessels is remarkable. It is no wonder therefore that the story of their exploits is still talked about in both countries. Overseas family members, descendants of those intrepid sailors, are all rightly proud of their Manx ancestry.

Vixen, being the first Manx vessel to make the journey, and being such a progressive venture, is well remembered. There are many relatives of the 37 adventurers alive today and various items and memorabilia still exist. Of interest are two linen shirts made for John (Juan) Watterson who wore them to Australia and which returned with him to Peel. They were presented to the Manx Museum in 1952 by his niece, Isabel Moughtin of Peel, and one of them is currently on display in the Manx Museum.

Thomas Joshua Graves' headstone in Peel new cemetery has a panel depicting the departure of *Vixen* in 1853. A more modern representation is the limited edition glass model of *Vixen*, made in 1979 (Fig 56).

The adventurers had mixed fortunes in the Australian goldfields, but Ballarat Terrace, a terrace of houses on Peveril Road, Peel, was probably named in anticipation of great riches being found (number 7 on Fig 2). Peveril Road, Peveril Terrace and Peveril Avenue are all in the same area

Fig 56. Limited edition glass model of *Vixen*. Photograph by Bill Quine of the model belonging to Ray Gell.

of Peel. Rather than being named after the cutter *Peveril*, they are more likely to refer to Sir Walter Scott's novel *Peveril of the Peak* which was first published in 1823 and which has many references to the Isle of Man including Fenella, the daughter of Edward Christian, a Manx Deemster or judge. It is assumed that Fenella beach is named after her (Fig 2). Peveril Terrace has been dated to 1840, so clearly was built before the cutter sailed for Australia in 1854. Another Peveril Terrace is in Wharekuri, Otago, in New Zealand's South Island which was the home of William James Cain (see Appendix 5). The building housing the Peveril public house (number 6, Fig 2) also pre-dates 1854, but the name 'Peveril' only appears after about 1857. At this time the licensee was William Clark, the father of Ann Clark who later married Thomas Mylchreest (see page 80). It is fair to assume therefore that this Peveril name relates to the cutter.

Fig 57. Photo montage of Peveril place names in Peel. For locations see Fig 2. Photographs Vic Bates and Barbara Greenwood

There are many other Peveril place names worldwide, but probably all refer to *Peveril of the Peak*. There are far fewer *Vixen* references, and sadly the successful Melbourne Vixen's netball team must surely refer to the female fox.

In Queensland, Captain John Mylchreest's name lives on in Mylchreest Street in Manunda, a suburb of Cairns. This has become something of a Mecca and photo opportunity for visiting Mylchreests (Fig 58) since Brian Mylchreest first 'discovered' it in the 1980s. At that time it was spelt incorrectly with only one 'e', now thankfully corrected.

Chrissie Mylchreest's first husband, Henry Simmonds, was influential in Gordonvale outside Cairns, and the naming of Simmonds Street there is testimony to this (Fig 59).

It is hoped that anyone reading this with links to either Australia or the Isle of Man will be interested enough to look further at the history of nineteenth-century pioneering adventure, daring and exploration.

Fig 58 Mylchreest Street in Cairns. Seven direct descendants of John and Christian Mylchreest of Peel, October 2015.
© Barbara Greenwood

Fig 59 Simmonds Street in Gordonvale, October 2015. Maree Reghenzani (née Simmonds) left, Brett and Haylee Simmonds.
© Barbara Greenwood

Sources and Acknowledgements

THE DIGITAL COLLECTION of the State Library of Victoria (SLV) in Melbourne is vast. There are over 200,000 images which are freely available and out of copyright. Images from the library are reproduced here courtesy of the SLV. Trove is a wonderful resource relating to all things Australian, created and maintained by the National Library of Australia (NLA). Extensive use was made of the digitised newspapers from which over 100 million articles are available. Newspaper articles found in Trove are reproduced here courtesy of the NLA.

The British Board of Trade required (and still require) that ships' Masters kept records of their crew and made returns every six months or on completion of an overseas voyage. Many of these documents are preserved and lodged with local record offices. The library of Manx National Heritage (MNH) has extensive lists of Manx registered ships from 1863 with less complete coverage of earlier lists. The Crew List Index Project (CLIP) was set up nationally to transcribe these lists, and thanks are due to the volunteers who made their database available online. MNH has digitised over 400,000 pages of newsprint from 1792 to 1960 and these are available through their iMuseum. This has proved an invaluable resource, and extracts from Manx newspapers are reproduced here courtesy of MNH.

Grateful thanks are given to Bill Quine and Vic Bates who have been endlessly patient with my queries, provided photographs and made helpful comments on the manuscript. Additional thanks are due to Vic whose skilful work has produced the maps. The Peel Heritage Trust has generously provided financial backing to the project. Anna Goddard and her staff at Carnegie Publishing are thanked for bringing the book to fruition.

It has been a pleasure working with the extended Mylchreest family both in the Isle of Man and Australia, all of whom have been extremely helpful. My immediate family, especially husband Eric, must be thanked for their help, encouragement and support throughout the project. Our daughter, Dr Emma Greenwood, has provided much help with style and copyright issues. Thanks to one and all.

References

Docker, E. W., *The Blackbirders: A Brutal Story of the Kanaka Slave-Trade* (London: Angus & Robertson, 1981)

Flett, J., *The History of Gold Discovery in Victoria* (Melbourne: Hawthorn Press, 1970)

Graves, F. S., The Story of the *Vixen, Isle of Man Natural History and Antiquarian Society,* Vol vii (1968) pp 201–31

Jones, D., *Trinity Phoenix, a History of Cairns* (Cairns: *Cairns Post*, 1976)

Mylchreest, J. B., *The Sailing Ships of Peel and the Mylchreest connection* (Privately circulated, 1989)

Mylchreest, J. B., *The Diamond King. The Story of Joseph Mylchreest and the Mylchreests of Peel* (Isle of Man: Amulee Publications, 1993)

Pixley, N. S., *Pearlers of North Australia: the Romantic Story of the Diving Fleets.* (Royal Society of Queensland: Presidential Address, 1971)

Quine, B. & Bates, V., *Peel: A Slice of Time* (Isle of Man: Peel Heritage Trust & Peel City Guardian, 2011)

Serle, G., *The Golden Age: A History of the Colony of Victoria, 1851–1861.* (Melbourne: Melbourne University Press, 1963)

Slater, I., *Royal National Commercial Directory of the Isle of Man* (Privately printed, Manchester and London, 1857)

Stone, P., *Encyclopaedia of Australian Shipwrecks* (Yarram, Australia: Oceans Enterprise, 2006)

Taylor, R., *Straight through from London* (Christchurch: Heritage Expeditions NZ, 2006)

Watterson, A., 'A *Lace Family in America, 1936*'. The History of Burleson online <www.burlesonhistory.com>. [Accessed 20 January 2016]

Williamson, J. G., The Structure of pay in Britain 1710–1911, *Research in Economic History*: Vol 7 (1982), appendix table 4

List of Appendices

APPENDIX 1

The First Gold Discovered in Victoria

Geelong Advertiser 25 July 1851
OUR GOLD FIELD. Eureka! We have gold – gold in abundance. The verification of floating rumours has come, and we feel now in a position to state decisively that which we have long hoped to lay before the public. In area, depth, and richness of yield, the Pyrenean gold field promises to be of first importance. Mr. Davis, of the Avoca, brought to our office yesterday, a beautiful sample of pure gold dust, varying in size from a pins head down to the most minute particles, found on Donald Cameron's Station, at a spot known henceforth as "Clune's Diggings". The gold is valued at sixteen shillings, and was the yield procured in an afternoon's work, with a tin dish, holding about a gallon of earth which was hand washed in the roughest manner, by pouring in water, stirring it in the sand, and then pouring off the muddy refuse, by which process as much gold is supposed to have been lost as was gained. For four miles round, the ground has been dug at intervals, and in every spadeful turned up gold has been found. Platinum has, we have been informed, also been found, sent to Melbourne, tested, and returned with a testimony of its purity, and a statement that it is worth Seven Guineas per ounce. Mr. Esmond and his partner Mr. Pew got their cradle into working operation on Thursday last, and from the quantities procured by the use of tin dishes, they may anticipate a rich harvest. On this one gold field there are eighteen men at work, and it may be as well to mention that it is within eight miles of the

spot where the shepherd found the specimen of gold which caused such a sensation a few years back.

Now then for preparation. In the first place, it will be useless for men to go up to the Pyrenees without providing themselves with cradles, a consignment of which we are authorised to state would fetch any price. Spades should also be procured in Geelong, they are selling at a pound a piece at the mines. Stores should be purchased here, as none can be procured within fifteen miles of the diggings – parties have to send to Burnbank for rations. Blankets, rugs, &c., of course will be remembered. The preparations completed, we will describe the route. From Geelong to Buninyong is fifty miles; arrived there, "Clune's Diggings" are about twenty-seven miles further, to gain which make for Clarke's, and from Clarke's out-station turn off to Coghill's – the "Gold Field" is before you within a short distance – work! and success attend you! Mr Davis proceeds this morning with the specimens to His Excellency.

APPENDIX 2

News from the Australian Gold Diggings

Mona's Herald 5 May 1852

The following is an extract from a letter received by Mr R. Crossley of South Castle-street, Liverpool, from his brother, Mr E. W. Crossley, who has been for the last two years in Australia, dated Geelong, Christmas Day:

As I have now returned from my second excursion at gold digging, I shall give you just some little idea of the success of myself and the generality of the diggers in this auriferous region. The first time I went away from Geelong, we started for Ballarat (the first profitable digging in Victoria publicly known), after a wet tedious journey of ten days, raining heaven's hard the whole time we arrived at the diggings with our party of four, worked two days, got rather less than 1/4 ounce. Started for Golden Point on the Sunday, two miles farther up the creek. One of our party, tired of gold digging, gives up and forfeits all claims, as by previous conditions made and signed previous to starting. Consequently, our party of three being too weak, we joined another party of three real old lags, and got into a piece of ground 16 by 24 feet. Went to work about four o'clock on the Monday morning, and worked until seven at night, and got two ounces, in high spirits; next day four ounces; next 18 ounces, till by the end of the week we had obtained 68 ounces. Worked at this hole for five weeks, and made our party of six £900.

Dug another hole, got nothing out of it. Our stores failed, water too; and all having the dysentery returned to town to recruit ourselves. Staid in town a week and started for Mount Alexander diggings, 70 miles further north-east into the heart of the country. Bought horse and dray for £40. One of our party, tired of the hard work, would have no more of it; said he could not stand it, leaving us five strong. Began to rain again, and continued night and day, until we reached our destination, wet beds by night and wet through all day. However in five days we reached Powas Creek, a new digging five miles this side of the mount. Staid here, worked four holes in the creek, two on the Red-hill. Got in about three weeks 40 ounces; thought that would not pay, so determined that each man should go and dig a hole in a gulley, and started on the Monday morning. We two new chums had to dig our holes in just the same time as the lifers. However, I got down with my hole, about 6 feet long, 4 feet wide, and 7 feet deep by night. Went in again next morning, and by breakfast time found a speck of gold, about the size of a pin's head flattened out. Set to work, rigged the cradle; got two ounces out of the first cartload; washed about four loads on the Tuesday, which weighed with the proceeds of Wednesday, gave us for the day and a half 72 ounces, including a splendid nugget of 40 ounces, about as large as a man's hand stretched out, and something in the same shape, varying in thickness from a half to a quarter of an inch; also a fine specimen in orange-coloured quartz, of the value of about 30s in gold. This looked like a good yield, which continued for ten days; and at the expiration of about five weeks from starting we again returned to town to spend the Christmas, with gold to the value of £150 each. In about ten days' time we start again, and I have no doubt of our success being as good or better than previous.

As to the general success of the diggers, I can say nothing further than its being an entire lottery. Some go and get from one to 20, 30, 40 or 100 ounces per day, and others get none, or barely wages; but the general average is good first-rate wages. You can with safety advise any of your friends to come, providing they will work, make up their minds to all kinds of privations, robbery and murder – not to commit the latter, but to stand their chance. California is a fool to this, either in the quantity got or the class of men here who would as leave shoot you as a bird. Last week over a ton of gold came down from Mount Alexander, under escort, independent of what came down by private parties, which might be estimated at half a ton, by parties coming down to spend Christmas.

I don't think I shall overstate the time in saying that at the expiration of two years from this I shall return to England to lead an independent life, with plenty. I am not over covetous, and not a great spendthrift; and the luck we have had so far is about one-third below the average. In the next hole to us, in the gulley, a 13½lbs solid lump of gold, and 7½lbs troy of fine gold was picked up in one day; in another hole a 30lbs piece, like a gun barrel and 22lbs, 11ozs, 4dwts was picked out in a day, and many a hole is yielding 6, 8, 10 and 20lbs per day. Should it be our luck to hit on a spot of ground like this, our fortunes are made, and then I cut it – and I think ours as good a chance as the rest; and the greater the numbers of diggers employed the grater quantity of gold will be found. In the adjoining surface ground to us, on the Red-hill, a party of three made 84lbs, 9ozs, 5dwts and some odd grains in ten days. Got up same day as us, marked out their ground same day, and all we got was about 10 ounces, so you can see the gold is not diffused all over the country in the same quantities but deposited in pockets here and there, in various directions; but a gulley running north and south is supposed to be the best, and the farer of the hills bearing about north-east. On the other sides I think it has not been found: if so, only in small quantities, compared with the other bearings. Harry has fitted a party out with all the necessary utensils, to pay all expenses, and to receive a fifth share, five in the party; but I am much afraid that he will be a great loser; not but what their chance is as good as any one's else, but it requires some labour to get it, and if they won't work, why they can't get it. Often digging eight or ten holes, 10 or 12 feet deep, some begin to fancy it is not their luck to get it, and return to town disappointed; but they that will persevere are certain ultimately of getting into it, and that in such quantities as well to remunerate them for all their time and labour. I expect to be about a month before I start again, and am consequently about to give up the retail trade, and what I do will be wholesale. I did not much like the party that I was with, and consequently have drawn out. I am now about forming another party, and trust for more comfort. At present no lynch law is in vogue; but La Trobe and all his commissioners will be of no avail when the tide of emigration sets in; and I expect California will be as far behind in her deeds as she is in the yield of the precious metal.

The *Eagle* arrived about eight days before the *Lord Stanley*, becalmed three weeks off the line, and one week in the straits, otherwise her passage would have been one of the quickest on record to these colonies. I went to Melbourne to pass the entries on the 28th December, and as I returned the steamer went along-side the *Eagle*, consequently staid on board about an hour, during the time passengers were embarking for Geelong. The *Eagle* belongs to Messrs Gibbs, Bright and Co of Liverpool, and she is, without exception, decidedly the finest vessel I have ever seen in the colonies; and the passengers appear to be well pleased not only with the vessel, but also the conduct of the captain and other officers belonging to her.

I have a thousand pounds in my pocket, and I have never yet regretted the day that I left England. It is only a great pity that the parties with whom I was to have come out with, and hundreds of others, could not dispense with the idea of leaving home and friends for a few years. Had they have done so, they could have had a good prospect of returning in the course of a few years with a sufficiency for a more comfortable life in their native land. I gave myself at starting ten years, but I don't think I shall be more than half ten for my wants. I have spent a better Christmas this year than last, but things appear to be upside down. Instead of sharp frosts and snow we have a scorching hot sun, the pasture all burnt up, with the thermometer standing at 110 degrees in the shade. Mr A. M. is doing very well, making what he never did in England – a comfortable living, and out of debt.

APPENDIX 3

Letter from Thomas Gawne in Australia

Mona's Herald, 12 May 1852
To the Editor of *Mona's Herald*
Sir, – I have just received a letter from my friend T. Gawne, in Australia, dated Nov. 12 1851 with a request that it be published in your paper. I therefore send you a long extract, leaving it to your discretion to insert or refuse it. Yours etc. John Kermode
The writer says:

1st. As to Religious advantages and protection, either Melbourne or Geelong have all the privileges you have at the Isle of Man, at churches, chapels and preaching-houses: in truth from a Bishop to a Johanna Southcoat's bearded followers, with all the protection a Christian requires.

2nd. A Farmer may find employment here in all the branches, excepting manuring and limeing, which will pay very well those that will attend to it.

3rd. All seasons of the year answer to come here. Cashen (miller) says even a fishing luggar might make the passage. My advice is to one intending coming here, to look for a good captain and officers, which is of the greatest moment: they will take care to have a good ship.

4th. As to produce, we can scarcely grow enough, or we would be rich too soon. A cart and horse will take from 15 to 20 cwt to market: a bullock drey will take 2 or 3 tons. Dairy produce we send to market twice a week, which brings chiefly 2s.

A labouring man that is sober and active, will get from £25 to £30 a year; his wife about £20 for keeping house for her husband; and if a son (10 or 12 years) that can just walk out and follow the sheep, from £15 to £20; with a hut, firewood, water flour, beef or mutton, tea and sugar. As to Methodism, it is in a thriving way, except the gold will affect it. The gold is 60 miles from Geelong, and all sorts of people are gone there: they get from 1 to 12 oz. per week, and some lbs. weight. There is a government escort with mounted police comes down twice a week. What would answer the best purpose would be a number of Manx to come all together and form a colony: it would make people always at home.

If you think this will be of any service to any of my old countrymen, you may publish it, if you please in the *Herald* paper, and send me one. Remember me to all inquiring friends.

Yours sincerely

Thomas Gawne.

APPENDIX 4

Obituary of Evan Gell

This obituary was written 50 years after *Vixen* sailed and there are a number of errors, such as the length of the voyage, items left behind and destination port.

Manx Sun 5 September 1903

Death of a Noted Manxman

This week we have to record the death of an old and well-known Manxman, in the person of Mr Gell, formerly of Knock Rushen and Ballaquane, Malew, who died on Saturday, at Southport, where he had resided for several years, in his 69th year. Mr Gell was born at Billelby, Dalby, Patrick, and for many years after spending some time abroad, farmed Knock Rushen and Ballaquaggan. In 1853 Mr Gell, with thirty six comrades, chartered the sailing ship *Vixen* of Peel, bound for Sydney Australia, and the party reached their destination after 971 days at sea. Capt. Corlett, who will be remembered by many as a commander of one of the Isle of Man Steam Packet Company's boats in days gone by, was sailing master. On the voyage, the captain and his mate were both stricken with fever, and as the two were the only men aboard who understood navigation, things began to assume a critical aspect. As a means out of the difficulty, it was found necessary to carry one or other of them on deck at times to take bearings, and give the requisite sailing directions. However, the voyage was completed in safety, and it is stated that the skipper of a vessel, which put into Douglas through stress of weather, and was bound for the same port, volunteered to report the *Vixen* when he got to Sydney, but such was the success which attended Capt. Corlett's boat that she arrived three weeks before the supposed to be quicker sailer. One who knew Mr Gell well tells of an incident which the old gentleman many times related, and which may be given as the experiment at Socialism half a century ago. Before the emigrants of the *Vixen* left Peel they arranged that for twelve months in the new country they would put all wages in one purse, and divide equally after all expenses had been paid. It appeared, however, that before the good ship reached the Calf of Man, the happy Manxmen quarrelled about the allowance of sugar, and this terminated their trial of Socialistic doctrines. Many little things had been forgotten by those responsible for the larder. When the time came for the first meal, the crew found themselves without table, knives, forks and spoons, but not to be daunted at trifles, they improvised a table and soon made wooden spoons with their pocket knives. Another part of the Socialistic scheme was that the 37 cargoed the *Vixen* with wheelbarrows, picks, shovels, iron bars (for horse shoes etc), and last but not least, red Manx salt herrings, of which they had not a few barrels. All the above were sold at auction on Sydney quay and realised such fancy prices that the voyage only cost them £2 each.

APPENDIX 5

Biography of William James Cain

Reproduced under the Creative Commons Share-alike licence from The Cyclopedia of New Zealand [Otago and Southland Provincial Districts]. The Cyclopedia Company, Limited, 1905, Christchurch. The New Zealand Electronic Text Collection.

Mr. William James Cain, Peveril Terrace, Wharekuri, was born in Peel, Isle of Man, and was one of seven school boys who sailed the cutter "*Peveril*," from Peel to Melbourne, in the year 1854. The captain of this small band of young adventurers was Thomas Mylechreest, eldest brother of Joseph Mylechreest, afterwards the Diamond King of Kimberley. The ship's company consisted of: Thomas Mylechreest (captain) aged 24; John Mylechreest, 22; John Cottier, 22; William James Cain, 22; James Moughtin, 19; James Waterson, 19; Phillip Gorry (cook), 16. There was much commotion the day the cutter sailed, and many amongst the numerous onlookers shed tears, at the thought that the lads were throwing their lives away; but on hearing this, the lads themselves only laughed at the weepers. As they were getting ready to sail, the boys' schoolmaster went on board, and said he was proud of them, and felt confident that they were quite competent to do whatever any man could do. He shook hands with all and wished them a good voyage. This was in the right key for the young adventurers, who gave their old teacher three British cheers, and sang a songlet composed by themselves for the occasion. In this they asked their friends not to grieve for them while they were crossing the stormy sea, told the girls that they would think of them when far away, and promised to write letters with good news for all when they reached Melbourne, that place of great renown, where money was plentiful and gold easily found. All which was somewhat in the spirit of the men who went with Raleigh to lord it on the Spanish main, or with Drake to circumnavigate the world. The only land the boys sighted on their way out was the Peak of Teneriffe, and then they fell in with the coast of Australia. When they bade good-bye to all dear friends the day they sailed from Peel Bay, the boys promised faithfully to send letters home by any passing ships, and had several letters written to send by the first homeward bound ship they should see; but though they sighted several they were not able to communicate with them. The "*Peveril*" gave chase to two of these ships, but they altered their course and made sail; so the lads gave up the chase as they were anxious to make a quick passage. One day just as the sun rose, they espied a large ship ahead, and at twelve o'clock they were speaking to her. She was a passenger ship, the "*Delaware*," of London, bound to Adelaide. The "*Peveril*" had to shorten sail while she was speaking to this ship, the passengers of which were crowded from the bulwarks to the tops. It was a pleasant sight to the boys, who felt as though they were in the pit of a theatre, looking up to the dress circle. The captain of the "*Delaware*" was very kind, and offered to give the boys anything that they might require; they did not want anything, but asked him to report them when he got to Adelaide; which he did. That was the only tidings that their friends had of them. When the "*Peveril*" made sail the "*Delaware*" gave the boys three hearty cheers, and the cutter lost sight of the ship by sundown. It was after that that the "*Peveril's*" troubles began. When they got into the latitude of the Cape, the boys bent a new mainsail, as they expected bad weather, which they got, and had to stow the main and bend a big sail. They had to heave-to the cutter under a double reef. This had to be done every night for some time, with only two hands on deck, one as company for the other. The sails were trimmed for the occasion and the helm lashed to leeward. When the weather moderated the boys set the mainsail, but to their surprise it was rotten in the seams. However, they had good weather then till they reached the coast of Australia, and they made the voyage from Peel to Melbourne in 135 days. Everything considered, the voyage was a memorable one, and is entitled to a place in the annals of navigation. Of the party, young Cain was the first to set out for the goldfields at Old Bendigo, where he did well as a gold seeker. He afterwards met the little "*Peveril's*" youthful captain,

Thomas Mylechreest, at Snowy river, where the two became mates in the fine old goldfields sense, and they afterwards worked together in the same relationship at Lambing Flat and the Lachlan. Mr. Cain has not seen any of his shipmates for thirty-nine years, but should any of them travel his way, and circumstances require it, he is the man to give the hand of friendship to any one of them, and that in a practical way, too, for they were all good lads. Mr. Cain came to New Zealand in 1863, and worked at Hartley and Riley's Beach, where he did well. In 1887 he went to the Waitaki to erect a punt for the late Mr. Christian Hille, and worked the ferry for several years. He joined Mr. Hille as a partner in the ferry, and eventually bought Mr. Hille's interest. Mr. Cain was married, in the year 1883, to a daughter of Mr. David Whittock, of Port Chalmers. He has resided in the Kurow district for thirty-five years, has been a successful settler and good colonist, and now lives in retirement at Peveril Terrace, Wharekuri, having, of course, named his place in commemoration of the cutter in which he and his brother adventurers sailed from Peel to Melbourne fifty years ago.

APPENDIX 6

The Foundering of *Vixen*

Manx Sun, 2 April 1864
Foundering of a vessel with her crew
The schooner *Vixen*, of Peel, arrived at Port St Mary on Friday the 25th ult. at two o'clock in the afternoon, on her voyage from Bordeaux to Belfast, with a cargo of Indian corn. The vessel was registered 86 tons and was commanded by Mr John Sansbury, whose wife and family resided at Port St Mary. Previous to sailing on Saturday, he prevailed on his wife to accompany him to Belfast, and about half past two o'clock in the afternoon he left the roadstead, the weather being squally and threatening. As the wind was blowing strong from the north, the vessel was not long in reaching the Calf of Man, and, as the master was well acquainted with the coast, he sailed up between the Chickens and the Calf Island. Soon after three o'clock, when *Vixen* was about two miles to the N.N.W. of the Calf of Man, and on the "port" tack, a sudden and violent squall caught her and threw her on her beam-ends. The sea became furious, and with a view of easing the vessel she was run up nearly in the wind, when her square sails filled aback, and she immediately went down in twenty fathoms of water; the master, his wife, and five hands perishing together. The disaster was witnessed by several persons, who were unable to render any assistance. The Castletown Lifeboat was conveyed to Port Erin on her carriage, and at once put to sea, but was too late to be of any service. Making a circuit of the Calf of Man, she returned to Castletown at one o'clock on Sunday morning.

The *Vixen* was owned by Mr Henry Graves of Peel, Mr James Turnbull of Rushen, and the master. It is hoped that the Underwriters will not consider themselves discharged from all liability by the vessel calling at Port St Mary. The master and his wife were the only natives of the Isle of Man. The seamen were English.

APPENDIX 7

Foundering of *Peveril* at Warrnambool

The Age, Melbourne Friday 10 July 1863

FEARFUL GALE – LOSS OF TWO VESSELS.
One of the most terrific gales we have ever witnessed in this port took place yesterday, and has resulted up to the hour of our going to press in the total loss of one vessel and the stranding of another. The gale appeared to commence about 2 a.m. yesterday morning, for although the previous Sunday night was one of the darkest and most wintry-looking we have seen this winter, yet until the above stated hour there was no sign of any unusual weather. The gale appeared to be a perfect cyclone, commencing from the north, and settling down at S.E. When daylight broke, the bay presented a fearful appearance, the line of reef at the entrance being covered with foam, and the breakers near the shore being positively frightful to look at. The sloop *Peveril*, that well-known and favourite Warrnambool trader, was nearly high and dry broadside on to the beach, a few hundred yards to the east of the new jetty, and the brig *Golden Spring* was seen to be dragging. About nine o'clock the brig struck on the bank just at the commencement of the breakers, on the old wreck of the *Maid of Julpha*, and about one hundred yards from the *Peveril*, and the three anchors keeping her from coming any further, she was thus placed in a very critical position, especially as the gale appeared to be increasing. By this time a great number of people were

gathered together on the beach, and active preparations were at once made to rig a hawser from the brig to the shore, in order to save the lives of the officers and crew. The vessel was only about one hundred and fifty yards from the dry beach, but the breakers were so high that it would have been perfect madness for any one to have risked their lives in trying to reach the shore without help from those on the shore. A cask was floated off from the vessel with a line attached. This was soon caught hold of by some brave volunteers, who rushed into the water at great risk, and an attempt was made to get a second line rigged from the vessel. Whilst pulling in from the shore the line broke, but nothing disheartened, a spar was now floated from the vessel. After about an hour had been thus spent (the sea all the time breaking furiously over the vessel) a life buoy, with a line attached, was got on board, and one of the sailors commenced his short but perilous journey. The poor follow had been injured on board, having received a severe blow on the nose, so that when he was dragged on shore he was a most pitiable sight. The work of rescuing now went on bravely, and in a few minutes the whole of the crew and officers (9 altogether) were landed on shore safely, although in a woeful plight. As each man came on shore he was served with a glass of spirits, and a car was at once brought from the town by the police, and the poor famished shipwrecked men were driven into town, and left at the Princess Alexandra and Victoria Hotels, where warm clothing and every comfort was administered to them. As there was no hope of saving a particle of the *Golden Spring*, and as her anchors being out ahead prevented her from coming inshore any further, the spectators waited to see the vessel become a wreck, which she did in a shorter time than anyone expected. At twelve a.m. (the vessel having parted in two sometime previously) the main mast fell over the side, the foremast, after a few graceful heaves (as if reluctant to leave its lofty position), followed company, and in ten minutes not a vestige could be seen of the *Golden Spring* except a lot of floating wreck.

The Age, Melbourne Tuesday 14 July 1863

The *Peveril*. – The cargo was discharged from this vessel on Wednesday last. As a matter of course, the sugar, salt, and other perishable articles were completely valueless, and as scarcely anything was insured, some of our traders will lose rather heavily. We hear that Messrs Jamieson and

Co. had £300 worth of merchandise on board uninsured. After the cargo was discharged, Captain Poat had a force pump placed in the vessel, and she is now pumped dry. She does not appear much injured externally. On the lee side a portion of the copper has been wrenched off, but there does not appear to be any other damage. Captain Poat seems quite confident that he will get his favorite off safe and sound, and bring many a cargo to Warrnambool again, as in former times.

Warrnambool Examiner, 14 July 1863

The *Peveril* – This strong English-built vessel still remains in the position she came ashore, viz broadside on. Captain Chapman, her owner, arrived on Friday last, bringing with him several screw-jets and other appliances for getting the vessel off. He has no doubt of his success. The only injury the *Peveril* suffered is through a blow she received under the bows from a log of cedar floating from the wreck of the *Golden Spring*. With the exception of this, she has not started a nail. She has now been a week in a perilous position without injury, and only requires a low tide to be placed in a position to float out to sea.

The Argus, Melbourne, 31 August 1863

The *Peveril* – On Tuesday morning last, a final attempt was made to get this vessel off the strand, and the vessel was afloat. Just as she was passing the last breakers, a large wave broke over her, first snapping the chain cable by which she was being hauled out, and then the kedge, and the unfortunate *Peveril* once more was adrift at the mercy of the waves. A boat containing eight of a crew was also upset in the breakers at the same time, but all managed to escape. The *Peveril* now lies near her old position, but Captains Chapman and Poat still are sanguine about getting her off safely.

APPENDIX 8

Peveril and Pearl Fishing

Geelong Advertiser, November 15 1875

Mr. J. Small, a diver who recently arrived from England, and is now engaged on the cutter *Peveril*, at the Torres Strait Pearl Fisheries writes:

I left Sydney in the *Peveril* on the 19th June last, and after a long and tedious passage of 39 days we arrived safe and sound at Somerset, Cape York. With respect to the pearl fisheries, there are in these Straits about fifty boats employed, averaging about three tons each. Thirty of these carry a diver and apparatus, some two, and they belong to various firms in Sydney and Melbourne. Most of the boats have a crew of five men besides the diver, the crews being chiefly South Sea Islanders, and fine fellows they are in boats, I can assure you, the craft being kept as clean as a new pin, indeed a stranger would take them for gentlemen's yachts. There are hundreds of square miles of fishing grounds, and although but few shells are being got up at present, there is undoubtedly a rich field for enterprise. The vessels forming 'the station' for the boats are moored here and there under the lee of this or that island, and the boats are generally absent a fortnight at a time. When, however, we leave our ship we never know where the search for pearls will take us before we return, a roving commission being granted us, as it is all free selection, there are no vested rights, nor is the residence clause insisted upon. We let go our anchor in the most likely place, and down goes the diver. The depth of water here is from five to ten fathoms, and the scenery at the bottom is splendid, the surface is tolerably regular, studded here and there with coral monuments of various hues, intermixed with the fan tree and other vegetation, the colours of which are beautifully displayed in the great deep. Sometimes, however, I have had to cross blocks of granite strewn about indiscriminately, or piled up like so many cairns. Then, again, I have fallen in with caves and caverns which would have delighted the heart of a hermit, and in these I have seen strange-looking denizens in the shape of shell fish. Here, as contrasted with the waters inspected on our voyage, we always have plenty of company under the water, in the shape of fish, some of which are very pretty, while other ugly brutes remind you of the fictions of Verne and Victor Hugo. I was enjoying a long walk through one of the channels a few weeks ago, when I was very much astonished to see a large alligator in front of me. He must have been over 15 feet long. Now it is unpleasant enough to drop in with such sort of company on shore; you may guess how I felt when meeting the scaly monster in his own particular realm. He, however, did not condescend to notice me; no courtesies were interchanged between us, and I – well, I did not resent his want of common politeness more than by 'shaking the dust', or rather the water, off my feet as quickly as possible, and retiring to the upper regions. Shortly after this rencontre, I dropped in with another ugly customer – not a veritable sea serpent, but something very like one. I was walking along over a smooth bottom, when I saw what appeared to be a very large dead snake. I spurned the reptile with my foot, when – whew! – he came at me with a rush. Fortunately, my glasses were strong, as it was at these he darted. I drew my knife at him, but he got clear. I have often seen these sort of things before, but never had one tackle me. Another diver walked slap up to a large shark the other day as it was enjoying *a dolce far niente* opposite one of the before-mentioned caves; if he did not skedaddle up to the surface again it was a caution to snakes. Such are a few of the sensations we divers have to enjoy. But alligators, snakes, and sharks have made me forget all about the 20 boats – 30 out of the 50 I have already accounted for. The 20 carry crews of about 14 men each, chiefly natives of the islands in these Straits, and go where there is shallow water, say about three or four fathoms. A desirable spot reached, 12 of the crew dart like arrows down through the water, cleaving it with great rapidity, and it is highly amusing to see scores of heads bobbing up and down. These obtain large quantities of hacked shells, they work, say an hour, then sit smoking their pipes on deck as contentedly as possible. They are splendid divers, and can remain under water a long time.

APPENDIX 9

The Foundering of *Peveril* at Cooktown

From the *Maryborough Chronicle*, 22 February 1884

February 21
Terrible weather has been experienced at Cooktown. Twenty four inches of rain fell in twenty four hours, accompanied by a strong gale. The brigantine *Kate Kearney*, 69 tons, capsized and became a total wreck. The ketch *Rover*, 50 tons, the yawl *Lenton*, 23 tons, and the ketch *Fox*, 13 tons, drifted to the north shore, and are likely to become total wrecks. The schooners *Prompt*, 86 tons, and *Peveril*, 59 tons, drifted on to the bar. The schooners *Exchange*, 36 tons, and *Thomas Day*, 18 tons, were blown out to sea. The steamer *Corea* broke her moorings, and is now anchored in the stream. The Customs boat was wrecked, while the Pilot boat has sunk altogether. A number of other boats were either sunk or wrecked. Considerable damage was done to the jetties end wharves, and several houses are also damaged. The flood in the Endeavour River is the highest ever known. Great fears are entertained as to the safety of the settlers on the Lower Endeavour and Annan Creek. The gale abated this afternoon.

From the *Cairns Post*, 28 February 1884

The Recent Gales
The severe weather experienced in Cairns last week appears to have visited Cooktown with even greater severity, and to have been the cause of much damage to property and suffering to residents. The *Cooktown Courage* describes the scenes presented in Cooktown on Thursday as "a sight which it has not been the lot of any white man to have seen before." Footpaths were washed away, the torrents of water overwhelming, and carrying culverts and everything else before it; the telegraph line was lying all over the street near Armbrust's; the verandah to the Queensland Hotel was tossed on to the roof of the hotel; and every house more or less appeared as if it had been flooded. Of the damage done to the shipping in the harbour the same journal says:–

At about 1 a.m. on Thursday the force of the current, due to the fresh in the river, caused the *Corea*, to part her cables – large thick Manilla hemp – from No. 3 wharf, and she drifted towards the *Muriel*, then lying at the old jetty, cutting the latter vessel's head lines. The *Muriel* swung off, when the *Corea* struck her on the starboard side, completely cutting her chaffing spars and bulging the rim of her angles. The *Muriel* was then helpless, and as she parted all her cables, both steamers were taken by the current down to the pilot jetty, the *Corea*, besides dragging her own anchors, fouled with the *Muriel*'s anchor chain, the latter laid across the *Corea*'s bows. Both were aground near the pilot boat-shed, one on the town side, the other on the lee side. The *Murie*l lost both anchors and was disabled, her stern part and grating having been all carried away. The rudder was also bent and the propeller damaged. At 4 a.m. help was sought, and Captain Mackay rendered all the assistance he and his crew could possibly do. Another picked crew were also taken on, who occupied Mr Baird's gig. An anchor was taken to the *Muriel*, but she was in a bad state, her cargo having shifted to the stern part, and water all over her decks. One time Captain Brand had the greatest difficulty to keep her position and had very faint hopes of righting her. Her propellers are not yet in working order. Captain Mackay boarded the *Corea*, and full speed ahead had to be put on to get up to opposite the old jetty, the current being so strong. She was delayed from Thursday morning to yesterday, on account of bad weather, Captain McGrath not caring to venture out until the glass altered. It is very evident that ether the *Corea* or *Muriel*, from the damage done to the end of No. 1 wharf collided against the latter through the force of the current, but which we cannot say.

The smaller craft suffered the worst, which is principally due to the careless manner in which the schooners were moored. The schooner *Exchange* and ketch *Tommy Day*, both lashed together were washed away by the current from their moorings; they passed close to the *Muriel* and *Corea* about 1 o'clock. A light was seen in the cabin, and the vessels were hailed. From off the *Corea* pieces of coal were thrown, but no one answered, although a bailiff named Galloway and a Kanaka were on board. The vessels drifted towards the bar, but it is supposed that instead of going out to sea, both vessels have bumped so much that holes were knocked in the sides, and that they have sunk between the sand-spit and the rocky point, North Shore. During the afternoon of Thursday, Bauer's *Charm* was put out to look for them, with L. Bauer, W. F. A. Clarke, and two others on board. The *Charm* has not yet returned. The *Retriever*, we may add, kept her moorings very well.

About 7 a.m, the *Kate Kearney* had a "fit", and took to plunging and at last went down bottom upwards. Mr. Baird's gig, having been manned by some stout able oarsmen, rescued Sam Douglas off the *Kate* before she departed, and it is to be hoped that the *Kate Kearney* has now ended her days. The *Prompt* and *Peveril* dragged their anchors during the early part of the morning and rode out towards the sea, the *Prompt* bridging up on the sand-spit, and lies now in a listed position; the *Peveril* came to an anchor almost opposite the bathing shed. The *Fox* broke away, and brought up on the sand-bank, North Shore, but has since been brought this side; the *Lenton* was driven ashore and now lies broad-side on near St. Patrick's Point, while the *Albert* has evidently sunk in the sand not far away from the *Lenton*.

About 9 o'clock, the *Rover* went a-roving, having parted her cable and went at a race speed till she came nearly opposite the *Prompt* when she slackened; the latter vessel about this time made very great efforts to turn right over. The pilot boat and crew put off to board the *Rover*, which was done, and the schooner run ashore, where she now lies. Mr. L. Solomon, the bailiff on the *Rover*, was taken off just in time, and there was not time to haul down the distress flag. The *Spray* and *Mary*, shortly after the *Rover* went adrift, dragged their anchors, but, with the exception of some smart work to get the *Charm* out of their course, were brought safely to anchor between No. 2 and 3 wharves. The *Agnes*, the Harbour-master's cutter, was sunk, and a Custom's boat dragged its moorings until opposite Mr. Palmer's residence, where it now lies under water. The old *Lady Mary* through the antics of the *Fairy Queen* cut her hawsers, and drifted to No.1 wharf, where she sank and smashed to pieces. This is a loss to Mr. Stitt as owner and Billy Attwater as waterman. The *Lady Mary* is done.

The schooner *Clyde* (Captain Giles) which left here for Maryborough last Tuesday, anchored on Tuesday night five miles out, owing to the busy and windy weather. On Wednesday morning, the barometer still falling, she lay at anchor; and during that night a heavy gale came from the north, the vessel laying broadside on to an east sea; a boat was washed off the main deck, the bulwarks were smashed on the bow, the galley was completely gutted of every article, two hauling lines were washed overboard, and everything moveable was knocked about like skittles. The mate got his eye damaged during the gale. The ship rode with 60 fathoms on the starboard side and 20 on the port. After the gale the wind veered to S.E. Our informant says that during Thursday bullocks, a kangaroo, and a lot of drift wood went out to sea. The bullocks were alive, as was also the marsupial. An attempt was made to catch the latter, but success was not the word. A kangaroo hunt at sea is the latest novelty.

The *Cambrian Princess* experienced a heavy gale during Wednesday night, glass falling to 29–30; she rode gallantly, 120 fathoms having been paid out to the starboard and 90 to the port side. Captain Owens, who went to the ship on Thursday morning, reports having seen some twelve or more bullocks going to sea. The *Princess* is drawing 17½ft of water.

Much suffering and loss has been experienced by the selectors on the Endeavour and Annan Rivers, and many hair-breadth escapes from the floods are reported. A large number of cattle on the Annan were swept away. News from the Oakey states that four Chinamen were drowned there and the bodies of three of them recovered. Some of the settlers in that district had to take to the roofs of their houses for safety.

APPENDIX 10

Will of Thomas Mylchreest

Know all men by these presents that I Thomas Mylchreest of Glenaspet in the parish of Patrick retired master mariner being of sound mind memory and understanding do make this my last will and testament in manner following:

I leave devise and bequeath to my brother Joseph Mylchreest of Whitehouse, Michael, the whole of the estate lands and premises of Glenaspet, Patrick, also that house, shop and premises situate on the corner of Beach Street and Shore Road, Peel now in the occupation of Joseph Irving, also the sum of one thousand pounds sterling, the said sum being the amount of a mortgage chargeable upon that house and premises being the property of the Peel Parade and Land Company limited and numbered 5 Marine Parade, Peel.

I leave devise and bequeath to my brother in law Angus Clark, those lands and premises situate at Foxdale in the parish of Patrick and being part of Ballacarn[e]y.

I leave devise and bequeath to my sister Margaret wife of Daniel Sheard the sum of one hundred and fifty pounds sterling as a legacy for her sole and separate use and free from the control of her husband, and I further direct that the said legacy be paid six months after my death.

I leave devise and bequeath to my sister Christian, wife of William Callister the sum of one hundred pounds as a legacy for her sole and separate use free from the control of her husband.

I leave devise and bequeath to my brother Robert, of Cleveland Ohio U.S.America the sum of one hundred pounds as a legacy.

I leave devise and bequeath to Angus Clark aforesaid the sum of one hundred pounds as a legacy.

I leave devise and bequeath to Eliza wife of Henry Jones of Seacombe Cheshire the sum of one hundred pounds as a legacy for her sole and separate use and free from the control of her husband.

I leave devise and bequeath to my nephew Thomas Moore Mylchreest my gold watch, diamond ring and gold ring with Manx arms thereon.

I leave devise and bequeath to my brother Joseph my quadrant and sextant and picture of smack *Peveril* of Peel.

I leave devise and bequeath to my wife Annie for the term of her natural life the whole of the rents arising from my real estate all interest from mortgages and other securities and all bank interest.

I also leave and bequeath to my wife Annie the whole of the stock, crops and other effects that may be upon the estate of Glenaspet at the time of my decease, and also the whole of the household furniture in Glenaspet House.

I hereby direct that the legacies payable under this my will to Christian wife of William Callister, to my brother Robert, to my brother-in-law Angus Clark, and to Eliza wife of Henry Jones be paid upon the decease of my wife should she survive me.

I nominate constitute and appoint my brother Joseph Executor of this my last will and testament and residuary legatee of all the remainder of my monies, notes goods and effects of whatever kind, and wherever situate.

As witness my signature this 5th day of March 1890
Signed by the testator as and for his last will and testament who in our presence and in presence of each other subscribed his name
[signed]
Thos Mylchreest
John J Killey
Maggie Clarke

Selected Index to Names